THE RESEARCH-INFORMED EDUCATOR

THE RESEARCH-INFORMED EDUCATOR

Tools and Techniques for Effective Teaching

EDITED BY

MEGAN STEPHENSON
Leeds Trinity University, UK

ANGELA GILL
Durham University, UK

AND

ED PODESTA
Leeds Trinity University, UK

United Kingdom – North America – Japan – India
Malaysia – China

Emerald Publishing Limited
Emerald Publishing, Floor 5, Northspring, 21-23 Wellington Street, Leeds LS1 4DL.

First edition 2026

Editorial matter and selection © 2026 Megan Stephenson, Angela Gill and Ed Podesta.
Individual chapters © 2026 The authors.
Published under exclusive licence by Emerald Publishing Limited.

Reprints and permissions service
Contact: www.copyright.com

No part of this book may be reproduced, stored in a retrieval system, transmitted in any form or by any means electronic, mechanical, photocopying, recording or otherwise without either the prior written permission of the publisher or a licence permitting restricted copying issued in the UK by The Copyright Licensing Agency and in the USA by The Copyright Clearance Center. No responsibility is accepted for the accuracy of information contained in the text, illustrations or advertisements. The opinions expressed in these chapters are not necessarily those of the Author or the publisher.

British Library Cataloguing in Publication Data
A catalogue record for this book is available from the British Library

ISBN: 978-1-83708-241-4 (Print)
ISBN: 978-1-83708-238-4 (Online)
ISBN: 978-1-83708-240-7 (Epub)

INVESTOR IN PEOPLE

CONTENTS

List of Acronyms — vii

Foreword — ix

Introduction
Megan Stephenson, Angela Gill and Ed Podesta — 1

1. How Research Informs the Professional Development Curricula for Trainees and Teachers
   Angela Gill and Megan Stephenson — 7

2. Wearing All the Hats! Learner and Teacher Identity
   Samantha Wilkes and Suzanne Tomlinson — 25

3. How to Use Research to Illuminate and Transform Your Classroom Learning Experience
   Charlotte Wright — 43

4. Using Research For Adaptive Teaching: Responding To All Learners
   Evan McCormick — 61

5. Being An Ethical Practitioner Researcher: Conducting Your Own Research and Applying Research Ethically
   Aimee Quickfall — 83

6. Sustainability: Research and Reality in the Education Debate
   Leigh Hoath and Heena Dave — 101

7. Pupils As Researchers: Empowering Inquiry in Education
   Alison Griffiths and Jo Hopton   123

8. What is Evidence-Based Practice, and (How) Does It
   Work in Education?
   Ed Podesta   143

9. Becoming and Being a Critical Teacher-researcher
   Amanda Nuttall   169

Conclusion
Megan Stephenson, Angela Gill and Ed Podesta   189

About the Editors   193

About the Contributors   195

LIST OF ACRONYMS

BERA	The British Educational Research Association
BPS	British Psychological Society
BSA	British Sociological Association
CCE	Climate change education
CCF	Core Content Framework
CPD	Continual Professional Development
CoP	Communities of Practice
DfE	Department for Education
DoH	Department of Health
DSL	Designated Safeguarding Lead
EAL	English as an Additional Language
ECF	Early Career Framework
ECT	Early Career Teacher
EBE	Evidence Based Education
EBM	Evidence Based Medicine
EEF	The Education Endowment Foundation
INSET	In-service Education and Training
IPCC	International Panel on Climate change
ITE	Initial Teacher Education
ITT	Initial Teacher Training
ITTECF	Initial Teacher Training and Early Career Framework
NFER	The National Foundation for Educational Research
NPQ	National Professional Qualification
OFSTED	Office for Standards in Education
PGCE	Post Graduate Certificate in Education
PLC	Professional Learning Communities

QTS	Qualified Teacher Status
SEND	Special Educational Needs and Disabilities
SENDCo	Special Educational Needs and Disabilities Coordinator
TA	Teacher Assistant
UNSGDs	United Nations Sustainable Development Goals
	Intergovernmental Panel on Climate Change

FOREWORD

In 2010, the incoming Conservative/Liberal Democrat Government made reform in education a major element of its political legacy. As part of this refocusing, it was tempting to see a move towards a greater use of research in education, and in particular classrooms, as a positive opportunity. However, the model offered by politicians and their supporters at that time veered towards a quasi-medical model, with the creation of the Education Endowment Foundation and a research landscape dominated by randomised controlled trials and teachers as consumers of research rather than creators. This systematic revolution of 'medicalised' research in education ignored the complexity of schools and classrooms and attempted to disenfranchise teachers from becoming more deeply involved in researching their own practice, exploring and understanding the complex, local contexts in which they worked.

This volume is a positive contribution in presenting how teachers and teacher educators use the research evidence base provided by the DfE as a benchmark but also goes beyond, challenging a simplistic view of classrooms and wider educational issues and how we can understand and explore them as part of the work of professionals in education. Schon (1983) distinguished between the 'high ground' of theory and the 'swampy lowlands' of practice and questioned the degree to which the uplands were of practical utility in the messy world of the practitioner. This volume provides an excellent roadmap for exploring how these two different worlds can be brought together to offer positive opportunities for practitioners to develop an understanding of and practice within research to support the critical development of their own professional work.

Professor Phil Wood
Nottingham Trent University

INTRODUCTION

Megan Stephenson[a], Angela Gill[b] and Ed Podesta[a]

[a]*Leeds Trinity University, UK*
[b]*Durham University, UK*

We hope this book will enable teachers and teacher educators to re-address the pressing issue of the relationship between practice and research in teaching. The background to the book is the English government's decision to undertake a 'market review' of initial teacher education, and our increasing professional and therefore personal frustration with the narrow conceptions that the policy makers then brought to bear on the way that research, research evidence and practice might (and should) relate to each other. We have spent the last three years working in reaction to those policy decisions, and wanted instead to speak back – certainly to those policy makers, but also to colleagues and peers in teaching and teacher-education.

The biographies of our authors show they are grounded in many years of experience in the practice of classroom teaching, but also that they are at different points in their continuing professional journey and transition into higher education and teacher education (or training). Some were teaching in classrooms when the book was first discussed between us, some of us have been learning how to become teacher-educators for much longer! The book is therefore also a collection of different perspectives and approaches towards the contemporary issue of the relationship between practice and research in the field of education. This means that some of the chapters discuss issues in much more concrete terms, focused on particular classroom problems and dilemmas experienced in schools. Others ground their writing in the professional education problems that their current work exposes them to. For some, this means the issues of the contemporary teacher-education or master's of education seminar room – how to help trainees and teachers understand the relationship between initial and ongoing professional development and research evidence. We hope that you agree with us that this diversity of approach is a strength of our collective work, because each chapter brings a new opportunity to engage with the interests of potential readers, whether you are just starting out in pre-service teacher training, taking steps to develop your practice or career, or whether you are looking for ways to move out from under some of the dominant approaches and mentalities that are critiqued in the book.

In Chapter 1, Angela Gill and Megan Stephenson start the book by outlining different relationships between research and the curriculum and practice of teacher education. After describing an idealised 'cause' and 'effect' relationship that policy assumes, they explain how that has impacted on regulatory requirements for teacher education in England, and outline how providers of teacher education have tried to go beyond official requirements to provide curricula, experiences and practices that better reflect the way a broader research perspective has characterised teachers' professional development.

Chapter 2 brings a sharp focus on the experiences of new teachers. Samantha Wilkes and Suzanne Tomlinson use research evidence to explore the ways in which preservice and novice teachers form teacher identities in the pressured environment of initial education, training placements, and first professional positions. The fact that teachers wear 'all the hats' is a springboard to considering how this research helps us understand these different responsibilities and stakeholders, as a context for identity formation. The chapter builds up to a helpful toolkit for new teachers navigating these multiple pressures and demands.

In Chapter 3, Charlotte Wright brings together the themes of the first chapters to help trainees and early career teachers recognise the ways that different types of research can help them address concrete dilemmas they are experiencing in practice, including the way that research is used as a cover for imposing changes to practice. Charlotte's approach respects and seeks to develop teachers' autonomy by encouraging them to make evaluations of their practice and of research. This chapter also outlines concrete steps that practitioners can use and develop in their use of research, but always with an eye on the development of judgement and practitioner wisdom.

Experienced and novice teachers have consistently prioritised adaptive teaching and responding to learners' needs as an area where they feel research could contribute more to their practice. Chapter 4 takes the themes and issues of the book and brings them to bear on this concrete issue. Evan McCormick models the way that practitioners can use research literature to develop an overview of practices, and then focuses on how it can also help them develop specific aspects of their own work. This chapter places that development in the ongoing debates and dilemmas about purposes, impact and professional compromises that characterise educational practice, but also brings to the surface the different ways in which we can notice these dilemmas, and the impact of our practice. In this way, Evan's work encapsulates the call for 'systematic' evaluation of practice and the development of more 'intelligent action' that can result.

In Chapter 5, Aimee Quickfall argues for the importance of research ethics for teacher-researchers. Aimee explains the responsibilities for ethical practice of research in ways that align with the big themes of this book – teachers have to think about competing ends and means – the benefits and harms that their work might bring, and have to learn to notice these emerging as they undertake their work. Aimee's argument is that this focus brings development opportunities for researchers – that ethical research is always better research. The book as a whole also argues that this enhanced awareness brings benefits for practice. The relationship between ethics and practice is reinforced by Aimee's explanation of the key ethical issues through clear real-world examples and case studies.

Leigh Hoath and Heena Dave, in Chapter 6, use research to argue that the issue of sustainability is at the heart of pupils' experiences of and anxieties about the world. Their reading suggests that, rather than treating sustainability as knowledge to be taught or CPD to be delivered, the issue of climate change requires teachers to engage with research. The chapter outlines how this can help teachers to understand the history of climate education, the barriers that inhibit its impact and ways to address the contextual issues of their practice. Crucially, they argue that teachers' responses should not be limited to developing more 'effective' pedagogy, but should include curricular agency that allows them to change, develop and innovate their curricula too.

In Chapter 7, Jo Hopton and Alison Griffiths ask us to think again about who researchers are, in an exciting argument for pupils' active participation as researchers. This argument, for bringing pupils into the circle of their own learning, for showing them powerful tools for making sense of their world, and for advocating change, is something we think will resonate with practitioners. The chapter is another example of the ways that a broader conception of research and evidence can make powerful contributions to practice and the lives of pupils (and teachers). It is also grounded in real-world examples and case studies in ways that should help teachers consider ways of integrating these ideas into their professional practice and development.

Ed Podesta develops many of the earlier themes of the book in Chapter 8 by exploring the meaning of 'research' in educational practice. This chapter tries to avoid dismissing any form of educational research, but suggests that recent policy focus on providing access to 'high quality' evidence that claims to tell teachers 'what works', has been a missed opportunity. Ed's argument goes beyond pointing out that policy makers have assumed that medicine and teaching are broadly comparable. He suggests that they have also made important mistakes in ignoring the lessons from 40 years of implementing a strategy of evidence-based practice in medicine. Ed alerts us to the urgent need to create an educational discipline which looks at classroom educational problems, with the aim of helping teachers undertake increasingly 'intelligent action', rather than expect them to copy techniques with fidelity.

Amanda Nuttall's Chapter 9 underlines the concerns about the way that the relationship between research and practice has been prescribed and the negative impact that may have on research and practice. Her insight focuses on the role of 'critical' and 'intellectual' engagement with research, as opposed to the kind of 'technical' relationship envisaged by policy makers. Whilst this might seem like something that busy, or less experienced teachers might not have space and time to explore, Amanda's argument is that this approach contributes to professional identity formation, satisfaction and engagement in ways that make teaching a more sustainable career.

This book is determinedly practical – it is designed to help new and more experienced teachers understand how they can interact with research in ways that address issues that are important to them. It uses case studies of real teachers' development and reflection to bring these challenges, opportunities and developments into sharp relief, and once again underlines our collective commitment to avoid dictating practice, but instead to enable and empower professional development focused on teachers' needs, dilemmas and experience. It is not a book that will dictate techniques. It does not tell teachers 'what works' – for reasons that we hope become clear (and compelling), but it is a call for action in a number of specific ways.

This book started as a way for us to confront our dissatisfaction and discomfort at the way that the relationship between research and practice has been prescribed (and in some ways proscribed) by policy-makers and dominant voices in related disciplines or interested sectors. But overall, we hope that we have collectively made a contribution which helps a more purposeful and thoughtful relationship between research evidence and practice emerge.

1

HOW RESEARCH INFORMS THE PROFESSIONAL DEVELOPMENT CURRICULA FOR TRAINEES AND TEACHERS

Angela Gill[a] and Megan Stephenson[b]

[a]*Durham University, UK*
[b]*Leeds Trinity University, UK*

CHAPTER OBJECTIVES

In this chapter, you will:

- Consider how evidence informs and supports the content of the initial teacher training (ITT) and early career teacher (ECT) curricula.
- Explore what high-quality curricula that encourage research-informed approaches to teaching and learning look like.
- Learn about how research literature has been interpreted in policy and practice.
- Explore the benefits of developing research-led teaching and learning through communities of practice (CoPs) during continued professional development.

Keywords: Research informed practice; department for education (DfE); initial teacher education (ITE); initial teacher training (ITT); early career teacher (ECT); qualified teacher status (QTS); core content framework (CCF); early career framework (ECF); initial teacher training and early career framework (ITT/ECF); continual professional development (CPD)

INTRODUCTION

This chapter introduces the core statutory framework that provides the foundational evidence base for ITT and ECT Training programmes in England, the Initial Teacher Training and Early Career Framework (ITTECF) (DfE, 2024). It considers the research and evidence base that informs the content of the ITT and ECT curricula. It explores what high-quality ITT and ECT curricula that encourage a wide, research-informed approach to teaching and learning look like.

The statements within the ITTECF (DfE, 2024) setting out the foundational concepts of how trainees and teachers learn and the pedagogical delivery will be explored. The chapter then takes a more in-depth review of additional research, through the work of Clarke and Hollingsworth (2002). Analysis and exemplification materials demonstrate how using wider research can promote deeper learning.

Finally, the chapter introduces a discussion on the benefits of developing research-led teaching and learning through communities of practice (CoPs) (Lave & Wenger, 1991). An example case study illuminates how impactful and effective continual professional development (CPD) can be for practising teachers when delivered by research-informed academic experts.

THE ITT AND ECT CURRICULA

Since 2016, there have been a number of documents published by the Department for Education (DfE) that identify what must be included by providers when delivering training in initial teacher education (ITT) and Early Career Education. In September 2025, the ITTECF (DfE, 2024) became statutory. The framework divides the curriculum into eight 'standards' – and outlines key learning objectives. The format of the framework closely mirrors that of the Teachers' Standards (DfE, 2021). 'The Teachers' Standards are used to assess all trainees working towards QTS, and all those completing their statutory induction period' (DfE, 2021, p. 3).

These standards set the minimum requirements for teachers' practice and conduct. The eight 'standards' are below:

1. *High Expectations (Standard 1 – 'Set high expectations')*
2. *How Pupils Learn (Standard 2 – 'Promote good progress')*
3. *Subject and Curriculum (Standard 3 – 'Demonstrate good subject and curriculum knowledge')*
4. *Classroom Practice (Standard 4 – 'Plan and teach well-structured lessons')*
5. *Adaptive Teaching (Standard 5 – 'Adapt teaching')*
6. *Assessment (Standard 6 – 'Make accurate and productive use of assessment')*
7. *Managing Behaviour (Standard 7 – 'Manage behaviour effectively')*
8. *Professional Behaviours (Standard 8 – 'Fulfil wider professional responsibilities').*

(DfE, 2024)

Each training route and provider in England is required to teach programmes designed to teach the 'Learn that …' and 'Learn how to …' criteria (DfE, 2024, p. 11). The DfE asserts that these statements have been drawn up using research evidence which indicates 'what makes great teaching' (DfE, 2024, p. 35).

The ITTECF is not a full curriculum but is the minimum entitlement that trainee teachers and ECTs are entitled to access. ITT providers and ECT training providers must offer additional analysis and critique of theory, research, and expert practice, as they deem appropriate for their curriculum (DfE, 2024). Each provider will do this in ways that demonstrate they are identifying key aspects of relevant research that underpin their modules. For example, providers often extend their materials from a wider evidence base beyond that included in the ITTECF when delivering programmes with the Qualified Teacher Status (QTS) qualification. Here they might focus in depth on further subject or phase-specific content, SEND and/or inclusion. By expanding the evidence base that is presented within the ITTECF, providers put forward a more comprehensive and tailored training curriculum.

RESEARCH EVIDENCE AND THE ITT AND ECT CURRICULA

According to the DfE (2024, p. 4), 'the ITTECF, is based on the best available evidence from this country and around the world, assured by the Education Endowment Foundation (EEF)'. The EEF is an independent charity that focusses on educational achievement for all pupils. It delivers research around key educational themes, and its Teaching and Learning Toolkit (Education Endowment Fund [EEF], 2021a) is recognised as an informative and accessible summary of education evidence (Stephenson & Gill, 2024).

However, the influence the EEF has on policy directives has come under criticism from academics in recent years. Ellis (2024) argues that the EEF must be viewed with caution, critiquing the heavy reliance on its narrow evidence base within the ITTECF (2024). Ellis questions the independence of the EEF, suggesting that pressure may have been put on its leadership to support certain policy directions. He also writes about discrepancies between the EEF's own research findings and how these are being used to justify educational policies. For instance, he highlights that the EEF report on cognitive science (EEF, 2021b) states that evidence for applying these teaching principles in everyday classroom conditions is limited, yet these techniques are being firmly encouraged when following the ITTECF (DfE, 2024) in teacher training frameworks. Hordern and Brooks (2023) argue that, as a result, the ITTECF provides a narrow and prescriptive view of educational practice, the impact of which may undermine teacher professionalism.

The DfE stipulates that ITT providers 'must have a fully developed, evidence-informed curriculum' (DfE, 2024, p. 5). As stated earlier, providers often seek to develop their evidence-informed curriculum across the QTS programme provision. Hordern and Brooks (2024) argue that this can be a challenge for time-poor and resource-stripped providers. They ascertain that finding additional research and resources to feed into the ITTECF curriculum, which closely aligns with the prescriptive document, can prove very challenging. Burn et al. (2022) advocate for coherent, research-informed, partnership-based models of ITT that maintain a strong role for universities working closely with schools. They express reservations about policies pushing to reduce or narrow the research base and theoretical components of teacher preparation.

High-quality providers 'integrate additional analysis and critique of theory, research, and expert practice as they deem appropriate' (DfE, 2024, p. 5) into their curricula. Therefore, those providers that build their curricula on wider evidence-informed practice can be seen to:

- Create a graduated curriculum, which introduces carefully crafted learning in steps.

- Introduce gradual stages of development into learning.

- Give learners the reflective tools and continuing target-setting mechanisms to review and monitor their ongoing progress.

- Provide learners with opportunities to develop critical analysis skills when reviewing the work of others.

The following section exemplifies the criteria in the bullet points above.

RESEARCH-INFORMED APPROACHES TO TEACHING AND LEARNING

Research-informed practice by trainees and teachers is encouraged and exemplified in the ITTECF. For example, in Standard 8 (Professional Behaviours), trainees and teachers are expected to learn that 'reflective practice, supported by feedback from, and observation of, experienced colleagues, professional debate, and learning from educational research, is also likely to support improvement' (DfE, 2024, p. 26). Oliver (2024) considers that reflective practice in education 'involves consideration of your own teaching practices and the practices of others, open-minded critique and a commitment to adapt your approaches following reflection'.

In Standard 8 (Professional Behaviours), trainees and teachers are also expected to learn how to develop as professionals through 'engaging with research evidence by accessing reliable sources, seeking support for how findings can inform practice, and monitoring the impact of applications' (DfE, 2024, p. 26). Engaging with evidence supports teachers in making informed decisions to promote high-quality learning environments. Teachers will be in a much stronger position to justify and articulate the foundations underpinning their teaching practice and instructional decision-making (Oliver, 2024). You will find out much more about engaging with research evidence throughout the book.

> **REFLECTIVE QUESTIONS**
>
> - Why do you think it is important to have a range of research evidence within trainee and teacher curricula?
> - How can you begin to engage with the research?
> - What do you consider to be factors that need to be taken into consideration when reviewing evidence or research?

WHAT RESEARCH SAYS ABOUT HOW WE LEARN

The ITTECF document outlines that the 'Learn that ...' statements are 'informed by the best available educational research' (DfE, 2024). This research evidence is taken from 'practice guides, rigorous individual studies, high quality reviews and syntheses, including meta-analyses' (p. 5). 'Learn how to ...' statements are said to be 'drawn from the wider evidence base, including both academic research and guidance from expert practitioners' (DfE, 2024, p. 5).

How Research Informs the Professional Development Curricula

Providers embed this content into the continuous ITTECF curriculum ensuring those training and within the first two years of teaching receive their minimum entitlement.

Current thinking behind cognitive science deliberately steers how the current delivery of learning takes place. The ITTECF (DfE, 2024) advocates models that emphasise the imparting of knowledge by 'expert colleagues' (p. 7), whereby the learner takes this new knowledge and practices delivering it in the classroom. Here, they are encouraged to analyse, alongside their mentor, how theory can be applied in practice. When this process is repeated continually, it becomes embedded, and the learner develops a level of competency. Fig. 1.1 illustrates how this cycle of delivery takes place.

Clarke and Hollingsworth (2002), when exploring models of how trainee and in service teachers learn, developed a progressive nonlinear model of teacher professional growth. They emphasised the importance of considering the complex interplay between the

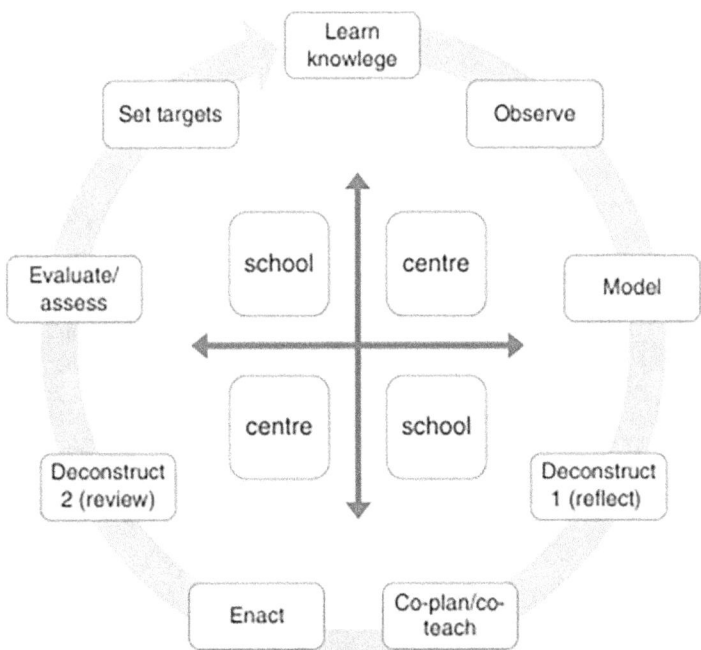

Fig. 1.1. A Carefully Sequenced Knowledge- and Application-based Model. Stephenson and Gill (2024, p. 20).

individual themselves, the context in which the learning takes place, and other systemic factors in shaping how teachers (and therefore trainees) learn. Their model acknowledged the influence of various factors on learning, such as personal beliefs, social interactions, and institutional support. As a result, the model provides further insight and evidence for providers looking to design professional curricula that go beyond the minimum requirements. Fig. 1.2 illustrates how the learner must constantly reflect on the knowledge and what this looks like in practice before learning becomes embedded and behaviours change. This can be a backward and forward approach.

A difference to note between this model and Fig. 1.1 is the two-way interplay between new knowledge and developing competency in practice. In Fig. 1.2, the learning moves backwards and forwards; it is not set within a continuing cycle of progress. It is through careful review and analysis that requires the learner and their expert colleagues to go backwards and forwards discussing and reviewing experiences, where true learning takes place. When

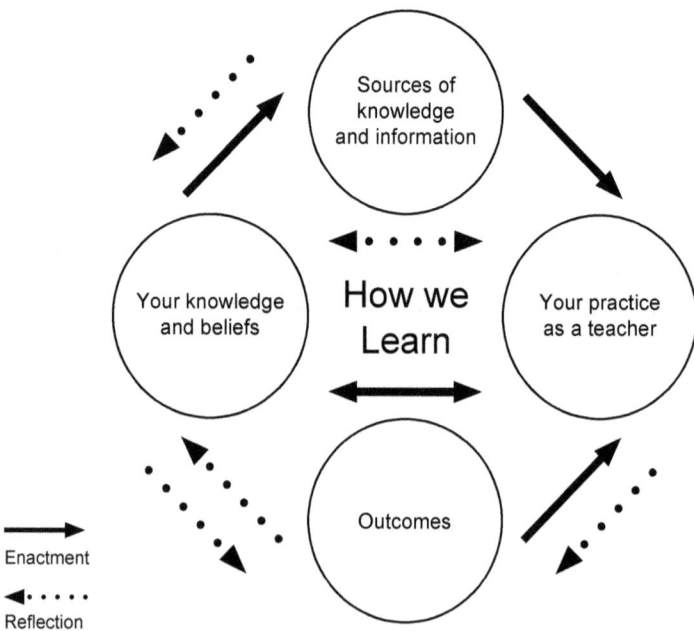

Fig. 1.2. 'How Trainees Learn'. Adapted from Clarke and Hollingsworth (2002).

this occurs (and this can be through trial and error), a shift in the alignment of new knowledge happens, and subsequently, a shift in practice follows. Sometimes learning can be a messy business! The more mistakes we make, the more opportunities there are to learn.

HOW CLAKE AND HOLLINGSWORTH'S MODEL DEMONSTRATES 'DEEPER' LEARNING

The key elements employed by Clarke and Hollingsworth are the emphasis on dialogue and shared reasoning. Learners are encouraged to exercise their own professional judgement throughout. An example of this would be the learner and their mentor discussing and dissecting 'dilemmas' and 'practice problems' (Burn et al., 2022). This dialogic approach helps trainees and new teachers understand how experienced teachers come to decisions within their own practice, and it goes beyond the narrow evidence base and development methods of the ITTECF.

Clarke and Hollingsworth's model suggests that focussed dialogue allows the unpacking of ideas and pre-conceptions, leading to deep, reflexive practice.

Providing time and space for trainees and teachers to engage in this kind of 'practical theorising' (McIntyre, 1995, p. 1), critically analysing ideas from various sources and perspectives, means that they can draw on current evidence. This evidence could be about pupils, models of learning, cognitive science, and also well-developed subject and age-phase pedagogies. Furthermore, this model encourages the unpacking and examination of knowledge in the context of the curriculum in schools, and the context of the trainees' and teachers' own practice.

This model of trainee and teacher learning and development also allows all to evaluate their own progress, beyond the statements in the statutory documents. Therefore:

- Over time, trainees and teachers become aware of, and talk about new sources of important information, about important things like 'safeguarding' and 'memory models', but also about specific ways of practice that your subject and age phase community have developed concepts and methods of teaching.

- As they think in more sophisticated ways about their subjects and teaching, trainees and teachers broaden their focus across the teaching and learning cycle.
- Over time, trainees and teachers notice new things in the classroom, such as pupils' thinking and breakthroughs, but also their questions, challenges and misconceptions.
- Trainees and teachers become more confident in making and justifying decisions about their practice.

There is a place for linear and cyclical models that suggest trainees and teachers 'learn then do' in their practice. However, in order to provide more effective and more interesting approaches to learning, Clarke and Hollingsworth's model provides a deeper understanding of the research into how trainees 'learn more and learn well'. This can be applied to ECTs and experienced teachers. It also allows us all to consider (and accept) the evidence behind the complexities and sometimes messy business involved when developing our teaching.

ACTION LEARNING SET

Consider a lesson you have taught that did not work out as you planned or hoped:

- How did you reflect on the reasons for this?
- Who did you consult/seek advice/share your disappointment with?
- How did your behaviour/teaching subsequently change as a result of your reflection on the lesson?

RESEARCH-LED CONTINUED PROFESSIONAL DEVELOPMENT AND COPS

The ITTECT downplays one further important aspect of professional development, and the evidence that goes with it – the way that pre-service and more experienced teachers learn in professional, socially mediated ways (Iredale & Tremayne, 2020) within

CoPs (Lave & Wenger, 1991). CoPs develop across learning environments where there is a commonality of purpose, values and a shared set of practices. Participants can continually improve their teaching practices and enrich their classrooms through collaboration, support, and knowledge exchange (Eraut, 2004). Often, the learning takes place in informal, tacit ways, through participation and collegiality among work peers. The learning and support networks which develop within CoPs are dynamic but vital to teachers' ongoing development (Reading, 2024).

High-quality CPD for educators enhances teaching and learning, improves student outcomes and supports teachers' ongoing growth and development (Coe et al., 2020). Recent policy in England has been designed with the aim that recently qualified teachers should 'possess strong mental models of great teaching ... [and also] have fluency in core practices and an ability to make good decisions to respond to the complexities of the classroom' (DfE, 2024, p. 6). However, Mutton and Burn (2024) write extensively about the need for providers to go further and deeper into the evidence base in order to promote teachers who are encouraged to explore autonomy in the classroom, becoming innovative thinkers and promoting a love of learning – for themselves as well as pupils.

CoPs are therefore more likely to be effective if they create supportive opportunities for sustained collaboration, give access to different types of expertise – practitioner experience and evidence-based suggestions for practice, common aspirations for improved practice and outcomes, and a focus on problem solving – learning through professional enquiry which is relevant to the challenges faced by the participants (Cordingley, 2015). This chimes with recent evidence that teachers' professional development is likely to be more effective (in improving pupils' outcomes) if it incorporates activities, structures and techniques which promote building knowledge, motivate, teach techniques and embed practice (EEF, 2021b).

Over recent years, the English government have continued to promote CPD for teachers through a National Professional Qualifications (NPQs) route. One of the programmes introduced in a revised suite in 2021 was an NPQ in Leading Literacy (NPQ LL). Here, aspiring or current English subject leaders across primary and secondary schools complete a programme to support their own CPD as English subject leaders. On the successful completion of the NPQLL, leaders are then deemed to be prepared with the knowledge and skills to implement and drive change and improvements in teaching, learning and assessment across the school.

> **CASE STUDY**
>
> The following excerpt was taken from feedback provided by a participant after they completed the NPQLL course at Leeds Trinity University. It exemplifies how the participant within the cohort identified the CoP that was built over the weeks, while completing the programme.
>
> As you read the feedback, consider how this individual:
>
> - *Responded to supportive opportunities for sustained collaboration.*
> - *Gained access to and recognised the value of different types of expertise.*
> - *Recognised how effective focussing on problem solving as a collective could be.*
> - *Applied professional enquiry to relevant challenges faced by herself and other participants.*
>
> (Cordingley 2015)
>
> Internal Feedback Received From Participant
Npq Ll (Final Workshop Session)
>
> ***Ques.1. How did you feel as a professional having the opportunity to share your understanding and expertise?***
>
> It was reassuring to know, as a leader, that schools had similar challenges and barriers. To start with, there was an anxiety that some leaders would be more experienced and be more confident or critical of your ideas. But as the sessions went on, it was good to see good and effective practice and share successes. A chance to catch up with everyone, and no one

judged your skills as a leader or a teacher. Everyone was there to support each other, and everyone was there to learn, reflect and develop their professional judgements and abilities. It was a chance to reflect on my leadership skills and celebrate the accomplishments and achievements of my team and colleagues.

Ques.2. What did you learn?

I learned to ensure the positives are recognised. Teaching is a hard profession, and sometimes we do not give ourselves enough credit or recognition. Everyone has barriers or challenges in their school, and supporting each other and sharing ideas can help each other as professionals feel better and reduce stress.

Ques.3. How did the academic team support your knowledge and understanding?

The academic tutors were incredibly knowledgeable. They recognised as professionals what it is like in the classroom and delivered the sessions with respect, professionalism, a sense of humour and recognition of contexts. They ensured we were engaged, encouraged our discussions, and supported us with a positive attitude to our assignment and case study reviews. Being able to guide us to updated academic research was a huge help, as this is something a lot of us have not done since university, so it was interesting to read new research and key findings related to literacy in education.

Ques. 4. How did the 'support' from the university impact on your experience?

Emails and communication were strong. Feedback was always completed within the hour of seminars finishing, and everything ran smoothly, which made the experience easier and something less to think about.

The excerpt above demonstrates the power of harnessing, respecting, and building on the experience teachers bring to a new learning experience. Continuing to develop knowledge and understanding by accessing research materials led to significant CPD and facilitated and nurtured deep, reciprocal professional relationships. This, in turn, added to the participant's feeling valued in their role and provided a continued level of job satisfaction.

All the participants had a commonality of purpose, by creating a safe space for learning and identifying the most relevant research the academics supported and guided how such could be implemented in practice in particular settings. The teachers were able to learn and share this knowledge with their peers through a professional subject learning community.

In summary, when implemented effectively, CoPs can provide:

- Enhanced professional learning and growth for teachers.
- Improved pupil achievement.
- Increased teacher retention and job satisfaction.
- Rapid dissemination of effective practices across schools/districts.
- Development of teacher leadership capacity.

CONCLUSION

This chapter introduced the core statutory framework that provides the foundational evidence base for ITT and ECT Training programmes in England, the ITTECF (DfE, 2024). It considers the research and evidence base that informs the content of the ITT and ECT curricula. It explored what high-quality ITT and ECT curricula, which encourage wider research-informed approaches to teaching and learning, look like.

The statements within the ITTECF (DfE, 2024) setting out the foundational concepts of how trainees and teachers learn, and the pedagogical delivery were explored. The chapter then took a more in-depth review of additional research, through the work of Clarke and Hollingsworth (2002). Analysis and exemplification materials demonstrated how using wider research in this field can promote deeper learning.

Finally, the chapter introduced a discussion on the benefits of developing research-led teaching and learning through CoPs

(Lave & Wenger, 1991). An example case study illuminated how impactful and effective CPD can be for practicing teachers, when delivered by research-informed academic experts.

> **REVIEW OF CHAPTER OBJECTIVES**
>
> In this chapter, you have:
>
> - Considered how evidence informs and supports the content of the ITT and ECT curricula.
> - Explored what high-quality curricula, which encourage research-informed approaches to teaching and learning, look like.
> - Learned about how research literature has been interpreted in policy and practice.
> - Explored the benefits of developing research-led teaching and learning through CoPs during continued professional development.

ACKNOWLEDGEMENTS

The authors would like to thank Sarah Bradshaw for providing her feedback comments in relation to the continual professional development she completed with her peers on the NPQ, delivered by Leeds Trinity University.

FURTHER READING AND RESOURCES

Education Endowment Foundation (EEF). (2021a). *Teaching and learning toolkit*. https://educationendowmentfoundation.org.uk/education-evidence/teaching-learning-tool-kit

Education Endowment Foundation (EEF). (2021b). *Cognitive science approaches in the classroom: A review of the evidence (summary)*. https://educationendowmentfoundation.org.uk/education-evidence/evidence-reviews/cognitive-science-approaches-in-the-classroom

REFERENCES

Burn, K., Mutton, T., & Thompson, I. (Eds.). (2022). *Practical theorising in teacher education: Holding theory and practice together* (1st ed.). Routledge. https://doi.org/10.4324/9781003183945

Clarke, D., & Hollingsworth, H. (2002). Elaborating a model of teacher professional growth. *Teaching and Teacher Education*, 18(8), 947–967. https://doi.org/10.1016/S0742-051X(02)00053-7

Coe, R., Rauch, C., Klime, S., & Singleton, D. (2020). *Evidence review great teaching toolkit*. Retrieved March 20, 2025, from https://evidencebased.education/great-teaching-toolkit-evidence-review

Cordingley, P. (2015). The contribution of research to teachers' professional learning and development. *Oxford Review of Education*, 41(2), 234–252. https://doi.org/10.1080/03054985.2015.1020105

Department for Education (DfE). (2021). *Teachers' standards: Guidance for school leaders, school staff and governing bodies*. DfE. Retrieved March 20, 2025, from https://assets.publishing.service.gov.uk/media/61b73d6c8fa8f50384489c9a/Teachers__Standards_Dec_2021.pdf

Department for Education (DfE). (2024). *Initial teacher training and early career framework*. Retrieved March 20, 2025, from https://www.gov.uk/government/publications/initial-teacher-training-and-early-career-framework

Ellis, V. (Ed.) (2023). *Teacher education in crisis: The state, the market and the universities in England*. Bloomsbury.

Eraut, M. (2004). Informal learning in the workplace. *Studies in Continuing Education*, 26(2), 247–273. https://doi.org/10.1080/158037042000225245

Hordern, J., & Brooks, C. (2023). The core content framework and the 'new science' of educational research. *Oxford Review of Education*, 49(6), 800–818. https://doi.org/10.1080/03054985.2023.2182768

Hordern, J., & Brooks, C. (2024). Towards instrumental trainability in England? The 'official pedagogy' of the core content framework. *British Journal of Educational Studies*, 72(1), 5–22. https://doi.org/10.1080/00071005.2023.2255894

Iredale, A., & Tremayne, D. (2020). Professional Learning Communities as sites for Teacher Learning. In L. Beckett (Ed.), *Research-Informed Teacher Learning Critical Perspectives on Theory, Research and Practice* (1st ed). Routledge.

Lave, J., & Wenger, E. (1991). *Situated learning legitimate peripheral participation.* Cambridge University Press.

McIntyre, D. (1995). Initial teacher education as practical theorising: A response to Paul Hirst. *British Journal of Educational Studies, 43*(4), 365–383.

Mutton, T., & Burn, K. (2024). Does initial teacher education (in England) have a future? *Journal of Education for Teaching, 50*(2), 214–232. https://doi.org/10.1080/02607476.2024.2306829

Oliver, M. (2024). Learning about your teaching. In M. Stephenson & A. Gill (Eds.), *Training to be a primary school teacher: The CCF and beyond.* Learning Matters.

Reading, C. (2024). Making the most of professional networks and your next steps. In M. Stephenson & A. Gill (Eds.), *Training to be a primary school teacher: The CCF and beyond* (pp. 289–309). Learning Matters.

Stephenson, M., & Gill, A. (2024). *Training to be a primary school teacher: The CCF and beyond.* Learning Matters.

2

WEARING ALL THE HATS! LEARNER AND TEACHER IDENTITY

Samantha Wilkes and Suzanne Tomlinson

Leeds Trinity University, UK

CHAPTER OBJECTIVES

In this chapter, you will:

- Consider why people want to become teachers.
- Explore what 'teacher identity' means and how this develops over time.
- Learn about the different 'hats' that teachers wear and how this differs depending on who they are communicating with.
- Learn how to manage developing as a teacher and being a learner, and how this refines throughout your teaching career to develop your ongoing 'teacher identity'.

Keywords: Teacher identity; learner identity; teacher autonomy; stakeholders – students, staff team, senior leadership, and parents/carers

INTRODUCTION

Everyone's journey into teaching is personal to them; it is important to recognise that some may have previous experience to draw upon, whereas for others, this is the first step into the classroom as an educator. The Initial Teacher Training Early Career Framework (ITTECF) (Department for Education, 2024) is the framework to support trainee and early career teacher development used by teacher educators. Before you read this chapter, it may be helpful to refer to *Standard 8 – Fulfil wider professional responsibilities* in the ITTECF.

This chapter will offer helpful suggestions on how to manage the varied and ever-changing roles of being a teacher. It will support your understanding of how teacher identity begins to develop. Your teacher identity development never ends; it continues to change alongside your knowledge and understanding of professionalism. Other chapters will also refer to teacher identity; Chapter 9 develops the theme and broadens the subject through the lens of teachers as researchers.

This chapter is entitled 'wearing all the hats', as this is what you will often feel like you are being asked to do. You will experience having to play many different roles in school especially in the early months and years, this can cause a range of emotions from exhilaration to confusion. Throughout the book authors note how the expectation to transform and be many different things within your teaching role never goes away. In this chapter we discuss the various transitions you may experience during your training and early years as a teacher and how, as a result your teacher identity will develop and shift (Beauchamp & Thomas, 2011). We review how you can use your understanding to support becoming the teacher you want to be. Also, we consider how to avoid becoming the teacher you don't want to be. Tips are given to help you navigate your way through the experiences.

There are many reasons why people choose to join the teaching profession, ranging from being inspired by one or more of their teachers to wanting to bring about change because of negative school experiences. The different reasons for wanting to become a teacher have an impact on your teacher identity from the very beginning. As you commence your journey of teacher training, you will experience changes in your teacher identity. You will observe a range of expert teachers, each having separate ways, means and approaches to teaching – these people will shape you as a teacher during your training experience.

TEACHER IDENTITY

Your teacher identity and agency are recognised as not being fixed, but something that evolves, shifts, and changes (Beauchamp & Thomas, 2011; Flores, 2020). These will be dependent upon many factors and are considered a construction over time, impacted by multiple facets. Giddens' Structuration theory (1986) discusses the ability of teachers to make choices and act independently, building their autonomy within the structures in which they work or live. To act with agency, teachers or trainees need to have 'knowledgeability' (Giddens, 1986, p. 281) of the structures in which they work; therefore, taking time initially to observe and understand the structures and stakeholders within the setting will support this. This requires working collaboratively with your mentor throughout, while you build and develop your 'knowledgeability' (Giddens, 1986, p. 281).

Becoming a skilful teacher will always be an unfinished project – a true example of life-long learning (Brookfield, 1995). Teaching involves problem-solving and having an understanding that your role will require you to have an element of adaptability, which is expected. Exploring your teacher identity and continuing to learn in this role will help with potential issues that you may face. This is an opportunity for you to reflect on your beliefs and practices, some of which may clash with the realities faced in school (Helsing, 2007).

A phrase such as 'wearing all the hats' can be likened to the changing identity of a trainee or qualified teacher, where there are many shifting and varying roles that you play within any one day or week. How you approach these roles and interactions can be complex and can be demonstrated through a growing understanding of the construction of the communities and schools in which you practice and are employed (Beauchamp & Thomas, 2011; Cowley, 2023).

How you build up your awareness and expertise to wear and change these hats, can be linked to your motivations and your altruistic driver to reflect your developing teacher identity and autonomy and to, in essence, make a difference to the lives of the students in your care (Arthur & Bradley, 2023) (see Fig. 2.1).

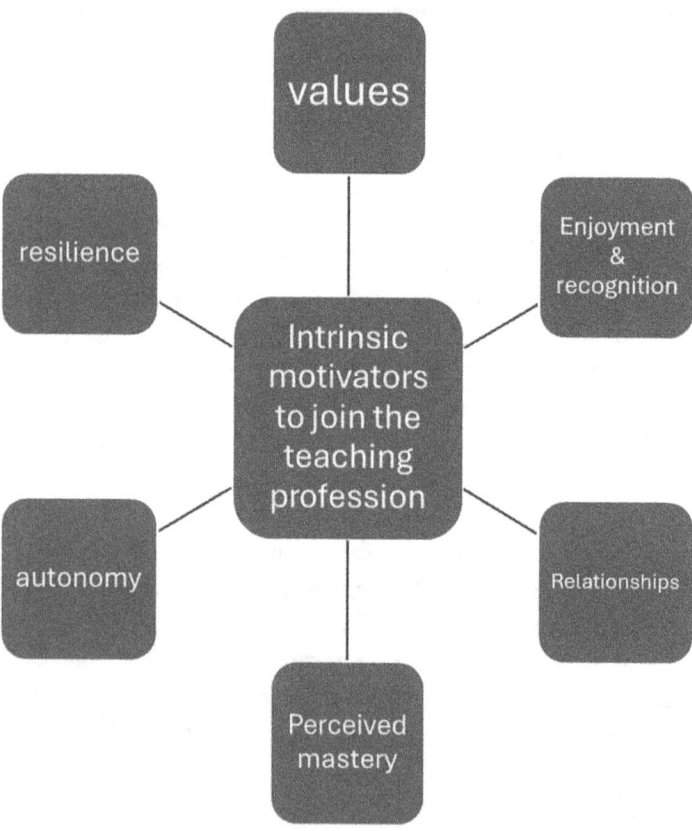

Fig. 2.1. Motivators for Entering Teaching. Adapted from Arthur and Bradley (2023).

> **ACTION LEARNING SET**
>
> Using the diagram above, consider what attracted you to the teaching profession.
> - Are the examples of intrinsic motivators ones that made you want to become a teacher?
> - What influences impacted on this choice?
> - What kind of teacher do you imagine yourself to be?

At the start of your training or as an Early Career Teacher (ECT), you will be asked, 'why do you want to be a teacher?' You will have many reasons for this, but more importantly, the question should be 'what type of teacher will you be?' This is not always a straightforward question to answer. This is something you should come back to and reflect on during your training and as you gain experience once qualified – this will ensure you don't lose those, often value-driven, reasons as you develop and grow as a teacher.

THE 'HATS' YOU WEAR AND HOW THESE IMPACT ON IDENTITY AND PRACTICE

As you gain experience throughout your training and early years in teaching, you will focus on learning all the key skills of how to teach, but you also need to remember that, as a learner, it is just as important to learn how to be a teacher. This is something you will continue to do throughout your career, and different experiences will impact and change how you are as a teacher.

The interactions that take place within a working day can be multifaceted and faceted. These can include in-person as well as through different mediums and channels, such as email, phone call and video conference. It's important to remember that these multiple interactions are imperative to the role you are playing. As a trainee teacher, you will be supported by your mentor and tutors through these new professional experiences.

Understanding and adapting across a range of different interactions with an array of stakeholders is a key element of establishing your identity and demonstrating professional behaviours.

Each school setting can function quite differently, and therefore, it is a good idea to first observe and ask questions. This will allow you to begin to understand the structure and organisation, as well as the number of stakeholders involved. This will take time but will allow you to begin to develop your role within this setting (Thompson & Wolstencroft, 2024).

Initially, this may feel like you have many parts to play and are wearing many hats. It is important to note that transferring between these differing identities can present some challenges, as well as creating variance and interest. Understanding how to make some shifts and adjustments is important.

It is worth considering the variety of different interactions that you may be involved in across a school day or week. These can be part of your teaching in the classroom, or they may involve actions across the wider school; all require a degree of professionalism as a trainee or teacher.

Consider the list below:
Stakeholders that you will encounter and work with:

- **Students** – Daily interactions with students are varied and key to building secure, respectful relationships (Wright & Wilkes, 2024). As these relationships develop, you will learn to adapt your teacher identity to different situations, from classroom instruction to playground duty, adjusting your approach as needed.

- **Staff team** – Professional learning communities (PLCs) play a vital role in school culture, fostering collaboration, enhancing teacher well-being, and supporting professional growth (Owen, 2016). You won't always get along with everyone in school; you will find some individuals easier than others to navigate. This is all part of developing your teacher identity and professional skills.

- **Senior Leadership** – Your teaching practice will expose you to different school cultures, some collaborative and others more rigid. Research shows that aligning with a school's ethos and supportive leadership fosters positive attitudes, collaboration, and teacher identity, while misalignment can lead to compliance, reduced enthusiasm, and identity loss (Flores & Day,

2006; Owen, 2016). You will begin to understand what 'kind' of school environment you want to teach in as you gain experience across differing environments.

- **Parents/Carers** – Building strong relationships with parents/carers can greatly impact your rapport with students and your teaching experience. Positive communication, not just when issues arise, fosters collaboration, supports student success, and enhances your sense of teacher identity (Quickfall & Wood, 2024).

> **REFLECTIVE QUESTIONS**
>
> 1. Consider a day in the life of a trainee or qualified teacher. During this period, there may be numerous interactions and events that occur as part of their everyday practice. Make a list of who they may encounter through this day.
> 2. During these interactions and interpersonal exchanges, how might their behaviour or their teacher identity adjust?
> 3. In relation to your role, how do you approach each of these different interactions across the day? How and why might they differ?

EXPLORING THE CONCEPT OF 'PRAXIS'

The concept of 'praxis' is the process by which a theory, lesson, or skill is enacted, embodied, realised or applied – [when] put into practice (Menter & Flores, 2021).

Menter and Flores' (2021) research identifies the interconnectivity of research and professionalism in teacher education, and how this can present some conflict in a trainee or early career teacher. This body of work reflects how teachers are often 'wearing all the hats' and how teacher identity can only develop and grow through acknowledging the everyday requirements of meeting the needs of all the stakeholders.

Here, you could consider how you begin to shift, maybe subtly, the identity you demonstrate when interacting with the students, compared to when you are contributing to a team or staff meeting, or conversing with a parent or carer. Simply put, you will begin to adapt your professional behaviours and how you approach individual scenarios with differing praxis, depending on the context, the setting and the individual or group you are connecting with.

Many trainees start their Initial Teacher Training programme with a pre-conceived idea of 'how they will be a teacher', with these ideas often disregarded once they join a school community and live being a teacher. **This is reflected in the case study below.**

> **CASE STUDY**
>
> Sarah, a secondary ITT trainee, shared with her peers and tutor how she was going to set her classroom expectations and how she would manage behaviour: 'I am going in hard, and I will be very strict, and I am not going to make friends with the students'. Sarah had previously worked in a school as a Teacher Assistant (TA) and observed teachers with a similar approach to teaching, which she felt had worked, for the most part, and the school had a strict behaviour policy that all staff had to adhere to. Sarah was a forthright character with a strong personality and did not like to be wrong. Over the coming weeks, as Sarah spent more time in school and teaching, she learnt that this approach didn't always work. Sarah reflected that she had to 'unlearn' all her pre-conceived ideas of how to manage a classroom and students, and took on board advice from her mentor and expert colleagues. She learnt that building positive relationships with her students helped get them 'on-side' for learning. Her mentor initially worried about her, as Sarah had such a fixed view on how to manage the behaviour of students. Sarah quickly learnt that her approach didn't work with the students she was teaching or the culture of the school, which used restorative practice as their policy. Sarah had to reflect on what she thought was her teacher identity and change this to suit the school setting she was placed in. Sarah was also learning to better understand how students respond to teachers and what they look for in a teacher to support and guide them. Sarah reflected

> at the end of her placement that she had learnt a lot about developing relationships with students and found that a much more flexible approach to behaviour can work. She also found it more enjoyable to teach than to treat the students like they were at a boot camp.

This is an example of how pre-conceived ideas can change once you experience teaching during your training year. During your ITT year, you are both a learner and a teacher, and for some, this can be exhausting as you learn how to teach, but also to navigate who you are as a teacher. One moment you are in charge and teaching a class of 30 students, the next you are attending a Continuing Professional Development (CPD) session on a subject you know very little about. An important point to note is that as teachers, we are reflective and adaptable practitioners, both in our teaching practice and in the development of our teacher identity. We need to develop the skills to be able to reflect and see how this impacts our ability to teach, be part of a school community, and still retain our own identity. Hence the term 'wearing many hats'.

DEVELOPING YOUR TEACHER IDENTITY DURING ITT

As a trainee, you can quite often feel like your teacher identity is lost among the identities of your tutors, school-based mentors and other colleagues. Flores notes that trainees sometimes report feeling like 'an outsider', as they are only in school temporarily and find it hard to feel part of the school community (Flores, 2004). He acknowledges that this can impact on them being able to find and develop their teacher identity during a temporary period throughout a school experience placement. Quite often, trainees are expected to pick up classes and teach just like their mentor has modelled to them. This can feel unnatural, as you are not imparting your own teacher identity into this. School culture can have such a profound impact on your teacher identity.

On the other hand, other trainees enjoy their placement experience and feel able to teach to suit their style, feeling compatible and well-suited with the ethos. The challenge here is the transition from one placement to the next. This is where trainees often struggle as they have 'learnt' how to teach in a certain way in accordance with one school and then feel they have to 'change' to fit into the next school community they join.

At this point, trainees can struggle with this transition because they feel they are becoming someone different again. As teacher educators, we see this as a valuable experience for many reasons, including experiencing a new school culture to help you decide what type of school you want to gain employment and develop in. It can also enable you to experience other teaching pedagogies from expert teachers. Helping you observe and learn strategies to develop within your own teacher identity. As trainees, you are learning the skills of becoming a teacher, beginning to understand the professional world of work, as well as developing your teacher identity and understanding the different facets of this. You are a learner and a teacher both at once. This can be hard to navigate.

TEACHER IDENTITY FORMATION: NAVIGATING PLACEMENTS

Navigating a teaching placement as a trainee requires organisation, proactivity and a willingness to learn, all of which help to develop your teacher identity and are a crucial part of that journey. Here are some key areas to help develop as a teacher, as well as develop your own teacher identity.

Observe and Reflect

Observing expert teachers helps you understand classroom management, student interaction, and presentation. Instead of replicating their style, reflect on what resonates with you and incorporate it into your own authentic teaching practice.

Be Authentic

As you develop your teacher identity, stay authentic to build positive relationships with students and colleagues. Be mindful of how your identity shapes your teaching and strive to create an inclusive, respectful classroom environment.

Identify Your Strengths

Take time to understand your own personality traits and strengths that can be incorporated into your teaching identity. Consider how these qualities can be used to engage students and create a positive learning environment.

Set Clear Expectations

Establish clear boundaries and expectations from the beginning. You will need to abide by school policies and curriculum objectives, but be well-versed in these so you can deliver them with confidence and consistency to help develop a sense of authority and respect in the classroom.

Adapt to Different Roles

Recognise that as a teacher, you will wear different 'hats' depending on the situation. You might be an authoritative figure, a guide, mentor. Learn to navigate these roles while maintaining your true teacher identity.

Listen to Feedback and Complete Some Self-reflection

Seek feedback, as this will provide valuable insight into your teaching style and help refine your identity. You need to remain open to developmental feedforward and use it to improve your practice. As well as seeking peer feedback, teaching is all about self-reflection. What worked well? What didn't work well? How did your teacher's identity impact this?

TEACHER IDENTITY FORMATION: MANAGING MULTIPLE ROLES AND RELATIONSHIPS

As previously covered, teachers interact with a range of people in many ways, from students to senior leaders. To do this successfully, you need to employ strategies to manage these multiple roles and relationships.

Professionalism

This can often be the most difficult to navigate as you learn to build relationships and to learn the etiquette and ethos of a school. Being professional throughout is crucial, especially when dealing with potential conflicts. Always check with colleagues and course leaders early on regarding the expectations, such as attending after-school meetings, arrival time for school, opportunities to meet with staff for feedback, even small things, such as dress code, can make a huge impact.

Personal Qualities

What personal qualities do you have that can be harnessed to make a positive impact in your role? Utilise these to develop your teacher identity and interlink these with your pedagogical skills to help manage the various roles when being required to wear various hats.

Communication

Clear and timely communication is key to building positive relationships with all stakeholders in a school setting. This can be from implementing the behaviour system, to clearly explaining the purpose of why you need a colleague's guidance in relation to your planning of lessons.

Support

When you are on placement, mentors, course providers, and wider school colleagues are there for support. Staff are willing to share their expertise and to support you in developing your teaching style, but this needs to be communicated in a professional and clear manner so that they know exactly what support you are looking for.

Self-awareness and Reflective Practice

Regularly check which 'hat' you are wearing and ensure that your behaviour aligns with that role. Engage in self-reflection and conversations with your mentor about your 'future-self' as a teacher so that they can help you navigate your evolving identity.

By employing these strategies, you can effectively manage your multiple roles and relationships with students, colleagues, mentors, and parents while developing your professional identity. The behaviour of trainees is shaped by a complex network of interactions within the school environment. Positive relationships with mentors, experienced teachers, and students contribute to more confident and effective teaching practices.

DEVELOPING YOUR TEACHER IDENTITY DURING YOUR ECT YEARS AND BEYOND

This can be a complex process that requires self-awareness and adaptability. Teachers adjust their identity constantly throughout their careers based on the context, audience, and specific goals.

Some key elements to think about when switching between different teaching identity[ies].

Understanding Your Core Self

Your teaching identity should be built upon genuine characteristics and values, rather than trying to emulate someone else. This will ensure that you remain true to the reason you chose the teaching profession, as well as ensuring that your teacher identity remains sustainable.

Be a Professional Version of Yourself

Your teaching identity should be an extension of your authentic self, not a completely different person. Wear clothes that make you feel confident, use appropriate humour, and share relevant aspects of your life with fellow staff and students. This will enable you to be relatable while maintaining professionalism.

Adapt to Different Contexts

Teachers often need to adjust their identity based on different factors, such as student age and subject matter. Be flexible and responsive to the needs of your students and the demands of the curriculum. A good example of this is that you may need a more nurturing identity when teaching Special Educational Needs (SEN) students, while a more authoritative one might be better suited to older students.

Practice Intentional Shifts

Switching identities requires conscious effort and practice, at first. Some strategies may include:

- Mentally preparing before a class to 'step-into' the required identity.
- Physical cues, such as facial expression.
- Modification of tone of voice and language.

Maintain Consistency

Maintain consistency in your teacher identity to build trust, set clear boundaries, and protect your well-being. Rather than transforming completely, emphasise different aspects of your personality to support your teaching goals and students.

Seek Feedback and Reflection

Continuously reflect and adapt your teaching style, allowing your authentic self to emerge while staying open to growth. Finding the right balance takes time and experimentation, so embrace the ongoing process.

CONCLUSION

This chapter has addressed the challenges trainees and early career teachers have in navigating their own path in the world of teaching to develop who they are as teachers, but also as learners. We have discussed what it means to be a teacher and the different elements that help define us in this role. We are aware that at whatever stage of your career – from a Stage One School Experience trainee to a second year ECT, that developing your teacher identity is a developmental process and requires change and adaptability when 'wearing the different hats', as well as the support from those around you and the school community.

You have reflected on your own teacher identity and what influences the way you teach students. You have also considered how you work with a variety of different people on a day-to-day basis, from parents/carers to senior leaders and how these interactions differ and which 'hat' we need to wear for which situation. This has enabled you to examine your thoughts, actions, feelings and reactions and the impact they have on yourself and those in the school community. Building on all the experiences and understanding the research that underpins pedagogy and 'teacher identity', you will be able to then understand how to create your own teacher identity and hopefully be able to answer the question, 'what kind of teacher am I?'

> **REVIEW OF THE CHAPTER OBJECTIVES**
>
> In this chapter, you have:
>
> - Considered why people want to become teachers.
> - Explored what 'teacher identity' means and how this develops over time.
> - Learned about the different 'hats' that teachers wear and how this differs depending on who they are communicating with.
> - Learned how to manage developing as a teacher and being a learner, and how this refines throughout your teaching career to develop your ongoing 'teacher identity'.

ACKNOWLEDGEMENTS

The authors would like to thank the editors for this opportunity. Also, we would like to recognise how valuable it has been working alongside many trainees who have shown us how to embrace the wearing of many hats, something many of us can relate to in our professional lives.

FURTHER READING

Quickfall, A., & Wood, P. (2024). *Transforming teacher work. Teacher recruitment and retention after the pandemic.* Emerald.

Rogers, E. J. (2024). *Telling their stories: A narrative exploration of student-teacher reader identity* [Thesis, University of Leicester]. https://doi.org/10.25392/leicester.data.27889833.v1

Rushton, E. A., Rawlings Smith, E., Steadman, S., & Towers, E. (2023). Understanding teacher identity in teachers' professional lives: A systematic review of the literature. *Review of Education, 11*(2), e3417.

REFERENCES

Arthur, L., & Bradley, S. (2023). Teacher retention in challenging schools: Please don't say goodbye! *Teachers and Teaching, 29*(7–8), 753–771. https://doi.org/10.1080/13540602.2023.2201423

Beauchamp, C., & Thomas, L. (2011). New teachers' identity shifts at the boundary of teacher education and initial practice. *International Journal of Educational Research, 50*(1), 6–13.

Brookfield, S. (1995). *Becoming a critically reflective teacher.* Jossey-Bass Inc.

Cowley, S. (2023). *How to survive your first year in teaching* (4th ed.). Bloomsbury.

Department for Education. (2024). *Initial teacher training and early career framework.* Service.gov.uk.

Flores, M. A. (2004). The impact of school culture and leadership on new teachers' learning in the workplace. *International*

Journal of Leadership in Education, 7(4), 297–318. https://doi.org/10.1080/1360312042000226918

Flores, M. A. (2020). Feeling like a student but thinking like a teacher: A study of the development of professional identity in initial teacher education. *Journal of Education for Teaching*, 46(2), 145–158. https://doi.org/10.1080/02607476.2020.1724659

Flores, M. A., & Day, C. (2006). Contexts which shape and reshape new teachers' identities: A multi-perspective study. *Teaching and Teacher Education*, 22, 219–232. http://dx.doi.org/10.1016/j.tate.2005.09.002

Giddens, A. (1986). *The constitution of society. Outline of the theory of structuration* (2nd ed.). University of California Press.

Helsing, D. (2007). Regarding uncertainty in teachers and teaching. *Teaching and Teacher Education*, 23(8), 1317–1333. https://doi.org/10.1016/j.tate.2006.06.007

Menter, I., & Flores, M. A. (2021). Connecting research and professionalism in teacher education. *European Journal of Teacher Education*, 44(1), 115–127. https//doi.org/10.1080/02619768.2020.1856811

Owen, S. (2016). Professional learning communities: Building skills, reinvigorating the passion and nurturing teacher wellbeing and "flourishing" within significantly innovative schooling contexts. *Education Review*, 68(4), 403–419. https//doi.org/10.1080/00131911.2015.1119101

Thompson, C., & Wolstencroft, P. (2021). *The trainee teacher's handbook. A companion for initial teacher training* (2nd ed.). Sage Learning Matters.

Wright, C., & Wilkes, S. (2024). Developing a teacher identity and creating professional relationships. In M. Stephenson & A. Gill (Eds.), *Training to be a primary school teacher: ITT & beyond* (pp. 47–61). Learning Matters, Sage.

3

HOW TO USE RESEARCH TO ILLUMINATE AND TRANSFORM YOUR CLASSROOM LEARNING EXPERIENCE

Charlotte Wright

Leeds Trinity University, UK

CHAPTER OBJECTIVES

In this chapter, you will consider:

- Where research is available for teachers, and what forms research engagement might take.

- How to engage in confident and purposeful critical reading to deepen knowledge of effective classroom practice and continue your professional and personal development.

- What does an impactful triangulation of theory, research, and classroom practice look like.

- How you might engage with research within school as a tool to help solve practical classroom problems.

Keywords: Knowledge validation; bias and objectivity; evidence informed/evidence based; critical reading; research

INTRODUCTION

This chapter offers an important reminder about the valuable kinds of research available to teachers and outlines what constitutes research engagement. It will support you in engaging with confidence in purposeful critical reading to deepen knowledge of effective classroom practice and continue your professional and personal development. It will demonstrate what effective triangulation of theory, research and practice looks like and give you advice on how to engage with research in school to add depth and breadth to your ongoing learning.

RESEARCH ENCOUNTERS BEYOND YOUR INITIAL TRAINING

The nature of your relationship with research will change as you move through your teaching career. At any stage, and in the different contexts in which you work, it may be more or less visible, more or less tangible in its effects on practice, and hold more or less significance in terms of its utility for your day-to-day work and conceptual development. Typically, the new teacher has frequent and supported contact with research through their training and early career years, where formal assessment measures might require its discussion and analysis and reading, or reference lists remind us of its variety, generation and influence over time. A little later, re-engagement with published research might become imperative for the teacher TAKING up a position of formal responsibility within a department, key stage or pastoral team, as they are faced with new, consequential decisions and choices. If a teacher chooses further study as a means of advancing their personal development, for example in the form of an award such as a national professional qualification (NPQ), a master's degree or doctorate, then research synthesis and evaluation is highly likely to be a formal requirement.

Research will reach you as a teacher in many different forms and through many different channels. In the staff room or school library, you may notice the presence of a collection of texts forming a professional development library for staff. In a department, pastoral or team meeting, your team or phase leader might share the latest research summary report, such as those provided by the Educational Endowment Foundation or by OFSTED. You may see research references on slides in a training event or find yourself drawn into a debate amongst research-quoting educators on social media as you glance at your phone. All these instances remind us of ongoing local and national moves to bring educational practice into a more fully developed relationship with educational research and could be said to represent important steps towards the democratisation of research knowledge. We work at a time when teachers are encouraged to see research as accessible, relevant and influential.

Yet whilst the 'research-informed' school is held up as an ideal, it is a challenging ideal to realise. For example, Proctor (2013) alerts us to the possibility of value-practice gaps in teachers' use of research: teachers may ascribe importance to ideas drawn from research but be unable to implement them, or may be tasked with carrying out practice or initiatives informed by research that they deem as unimportant or unhelpful. Research can be regarded as a tool to solve problems and develop knowledge and thinking, or a driver of imposed change, which can sometimes feel alien and imposed. Time and resourcing constraints may also preclude deep and critical engagement with research.

Another barrier to research use is when research and direct experience are perceived as somehow oppositional to each other. When you have pressing problems to solve or decisions to make, it's natural that the immediacy of personal experience will dominate your thinking. Yet it is important to pay attention to the limits of what we can know in any given context or moment, and to see research encounters as offering bridges into expanded or tested or alternative realms – bridges which could in turn help you to generate new or sturdier solutions back in your current context. A concerted effort to engage with research will enhance your professional judgement and help you develop confidence in distinguishing between proposals, initiatives and innovations in order to build the most robust and effective provision for your students.

REFLECTIVE THINKING

Research encounters can take many different forms, and can be placed across a wide spectrum of formality, with varying degrees of immediacy, apparent relevance, and practical applicability. If you were to list your encounters with research from the last 12 months, which of the following would feature strongly?

Mapping and defining the nature of your own research engagement can be a useful tool to begin to consider where you do and might use research to solve problems or validate ideas, and where that engagement might be strengthened or broadened.

Look at the following lists to create a map of your own research engagement profile. Which sources and contexts reflect the nature of your own research encounters as a teacher? Which might offer a new way into research engagement?

Sources	Contexts
• Research reported in the news • Whole school INSET or CPD • Formal or personal pursuit of key issues • Subject or phase specific, for example, EEF reports • Subject association materials or training • Education network conversations e.g. through social media • TeachMeets, webinars, conferences • Wider reading, for example, the staff CPD library • Academic study • Self-study	○ Informal or formal ○ Chance or planned ○ Individual or supported/group ○ Personal or institutional ○ Fleeting or sustained ○ Single source or multiple sources ○ Topical issue or pervasive education issue ○ Subject/phase-based or whole school ○ Local or national issue ○ 'High interest' (e.g., immediate impact/relevance) or 'compound interest' (e.g., part of a slow build of idea/information gathering/intellectual investment)

The next two sections will offer different ways into research engagement. Firstly, you will find a template for critical reading in the form of a set of stepped questions to ask of any piece of research. The emphasis here is on developing your confidence in taking on text types that might seem unfamiliar or far removed from your classroom. It positions you as a knowledge seeker who seeks to understand the parameters of research and to build critical experience in assessing what is being read in a general sense. Following on from this template, the next section also addresses the idea of teachers as knowledge seekers, and takes the form of a case study about a teacher undertaking purposeful reading with change in mind. As her own post-research comments show, the change that the reading supports is two-way: it impacts this teacher's practice directly, and it impacts her teacher identity.

ENGAGING IN CONFIDENT AND PURPOSEFUL CRITICAL READING FOR PROFESSIONAL AND PERSONAL DEVELOPMENT

A wealth of guides now exists to support schools in becoming evidence-informed. For example, the Education Endowment Foundation (EEF) offers support in the form of 'Using Research Evidence: a concise guide' (2024). This document defines what research evidence might mean, considers the kinds of insights it can offer us, and offers pointers for evaluating individual texts. You might also seek out the work of the National Foundation for Educational Research (the NFER), the British Educational Research Association (BERA), or the Chartered College of Teaching (check to see whether your school has signed up for institutional membership of any of the above).

A simple model of research engagement in school involves consideration of evidence, making decisions on the basis of that evidence, and then taking actions as a result of those decisions. Cain et al. (2019) point to the need for a more nuanced model, in which the teacher is given more status as a unique, actively thoughtful agent working and making decisions in a specific school context.

Such a model might include the following elements:

- **Expression** of context-rooted starting points: **assumptions, hypotheses, beliefs, opinions.**
- **Exploration** of evidence from sources **inside** and **outside** of the school.
- **Discussion** within the educational context/setting, including how **starting points** and **new insights** from **evidence align.**
- **Decisions leading to actions.**

As a teacher faced with the challenges of your specific context, engaging with research can enhance your authority to make decisions about practice. Chapter 5 provides further details on engaging in and with research to support your understanding of adaptive teaching. In choosing evidence-based strategies or reasoning informed by reading rather than a reliance on 'common sense', you can feel more confident that you are about to make the right choices.

Note – word of caution. *Not all research is created equal, and it's essential to evaluate it critically to ensure you're applying high-quality evidence in your work.*

Let's imagine you have been asked to work on a project to improve the educational experience, attendance and attainment of a specific group of students in your school, in your year group/key stage or in your subject specialism, or at whole school level. This could be looked after by children, for example, or those who struggle with reading. You've read relevant chapters from a couple of books on inclusion from your staff CPD library and gathered some ideas from a quick internet search for news articles and blogs, before deciding that it's time to delve into some published research. You can see that journal articles are available, for example via Google Scholar or a search for 'open access journals about education'.

At this point, it is sometimes tricky to make the jump from material explicitly written for a teacher audience, and that which seems to address a specialist academic audience. If your school or academy has a Research Lead, they will be able to help you get past this hurdle. If not, you might think about comparing notes with a colleague using the following steps to ensure careful reading.

Point 9 below offers a reminder that dialogue about any reading you have done will help you hear how you are summarising it for yourself and help you to determine decisive next steps.

BUILDING CONFIDENCE IN APPROACHING SPECIALIST ACADEMIC MATERIALS

1. Understand the Purpose of the Research

Begin by identifying the purpose of the study. Ask:

- What is this particular piece of research trying to investigate or prove? What questions is it attempting to answer?
- In what ways is the focus relevant to my teaching context?
- Does it address a gap or challenge in practice in my context?

For example, if a study explores strategies to improve reading comprehension, you might consider whether the study's scope and findings align with your students' needs, and how far the context or contexts in which the research was undertaken share features with your own.

2. Check the Source

Consider where the research is published. High-quality research is often found in reputable, peer-reviewed journals or reports from credible organisations. Be cautious with:

- Blogs, opinion pieces, or websites without academic backing.
- Research sponsored by groups with a vested interest in specific outcomes.

Look for journals like *Educational Research* or reports from trusted bodies like the *Education Endowment Foundation (EEF)* in the UK. Consider where and when the research has been conducted, and the authors' experience in the field, for example, by looking up the nature of any other published work they have produced. This is not to be dismissive of new work by new authors or teams, but rather to help you locate the study in its publishing context.

3. Examine the Methodology

The methods used in research influence the validity of its conclusions ~~for you~~ and its perceived reliability in wider educational circles. You might look carefully at:

- **Sample:** Was the study conducted with a sufficient number of participants to draw meaningful conclusions? Or if it was small scale, and data could be said to be representing rather than representative, what pointers or ideas can be drawn from them?

- **Participant selection:** How far were the contexts of participant recruitment similar to your teaching context? For example, a study on urban schools may not directly apply to a rural setting.

- **Research design:** Was it a randomised controlled trial, longitudinal study, or qualitative case study? What kind of data are generated by the method(s) chosen, and how accessible and useful do you find that data? Each method and dataset will have its strengths and limitations.

'Methodology' is the kind of concept word that can contribute to teachers feeling alienated from research, but at root, a description of methods is an important part of researchers' public-facing duty. In any study, the methods that have been chosen should be clearly explained and justified, and as critical readers, we should ask what kind of answers those methods were likely to make available to the researchers. For example, if in a study, the impact of teaching assistants is measured using teacher feedback and target student results, what might this make visible, and what other kinds of studies might you then want to consult to gain other kinds of insight?

4. Evaluate the Findings

Interrogate the study's results critically:

- Are the findings clear and supported by data?
- Were statistical tests used appropriately to validate results?
- Did the researchers acknowledge any limitations?

Remember, correlation does not imply causation. For example, if a study finds a relationship between technology use for reading, such as text-to-voice software and better reading grades, consider whether other factors might contribute to this outcome.

5. Consider Bias and Objectivity

Check whether the study appears impartial:

- Who funded the research? Funding sources can sometimes influence findings.
- Are the researchers transparent about potential conflicts of interest?
- Are the conclusions overly positive or promotional?

As a rule of thumb, a good study acknowledges its limitations and avoids overstating its findings.

6. Look at Practical Implications

Look back at your context to evaluate the ways in which the research might or might not apply to your context or classroom:

- Are the recommendations feasible within your resources and constraints?
- Does it align with your students' needs, socio-economic and cultural context?
- Is the evidence strong enough to justify changes to your practice?

For instance, any strategy requiring expensive equipment might not be practical for a school with limited funding.

7. Check for Consensus

No single study provides definitive answers. Research findings are more reliable when supported by multiple studies. Look for meta-analyses or systematic reviews that synthesise evidence from various sources. For example, the EEF Toolkit provides summaries of multiple studies on educational strategies, making it easier to identify broadly supported approaches. You might also look for studies with similar foci and research methods to compare the nature and reliability of findings.

8. Stay Open to New Ideas

Critical reading doesn't mean rejecting research that challenges your current practices. Instead:

- Approach studies with curiosity, considering how they might complement or enhance your teaching.
- Balance scepticism with openness to innovation.

9. Take Notes and Discuss

Whilst reading, summarise key points:

- What was the main finding(s)?
- How does it connect to your work?
- What questions do you have?
- Where will you go next, for example, to seek consolidation of any insights gained from reading this piece of research or to learn how different researchers have approached the issue?

Discussing research with colleagues can deepen your understanding and provide diverse perspectives on its implications.

Further pointers on how to set up this kind of discussion and take it further are offered at the end of this chapter. This may seem somewhat daunting at first, but once you become familiar with this process, you will find that using and evaluating research becomes easier, and that will, in turn, support you and your school's development through practice.

TRIANGULATING THEORY, RESEARCH AND CLASSROOM PRACTICE

Let us now look at a specific example of a teacher engaging with research with the goal of broadening her understanding and improving her practice.

> **CASE STUDY**
>
> Sarah trained as a teacher of Secondary Geography, having herself navigated her time at school with a diagnosis of dyslexia at the age of eight. Whilst she benefitted from strong family support and helpful teachers herself, she wanted to understand more about the varied and sometimes patchy experiences that her own pupils were having in mainstream education, and to view those experiences against a wider national backdrop of policy and available resourcing. The disparity between her own experience and that of dyslexic students in her care became a 'stone in her shoe' that led her towards research engagement.
>
> Sarah had gained 60 Level 7 credits during her PGCE and wanted to use those credits towards a master's qualification. The MA in Education offered by a local university included a dissertation module, and Sarah chose to explore research on the impact of dyslexia on secondary school pupils' self-esteem, with a view to improving her own and then others' practice. MA study outside of the immediate context of her school work offered the space and incentive to view the issue through different lenses, and provided a community of students working in different educational settings with whom Sarah could discuss her growing knowledge. Sarah's experience of Continuing Professional Development sessions in school on supporting

dyslexic students had been positive, but brief and scattered, and she used structured MA study to ring fence space to consolidate and deepen her own expertise over a longer time period.

For her dissertation, Sarah looked at research conducted in England but also significant studies from Australia and the United States, work by organisations such as the British Dyslexia Association, and peer-reviewed work by individual academic researchers or research teams. As her reading expanded, she began to notice which works received frequent citation and which ideas or themes resurfaced across multiple texts, and which were particularly resonant for her given her contextual experience. This growing understanding of pattern-forming and networks of knowledge enhanced her sense of confidence in her own expertise.

She found she became particularly interested in Lithari's (2019) work on the way that dyslexic students might experience a 'fractured academic identity' where dyslexia was framed as a difficulty or a deficit, or where students were pulled out of mainstream provision for support. This helped her form recommendations about the need for teachers to recognise the possibility of 'fracture' and take active steps to address it with dyslexic pupils, for example through creating check in points to talk about each student's unique talents and successes, and to discuss with them how any intervention measures were or were not working for them. As she developed a set of recommendations for practice, she also drew on research by Burton (2004) and Rowan (2010) around dyslexic pupils' self-esteem and beliefs about further or higher education being out of reach for them, Amran and Majid's (2019) work on the importance of stakeholder collaboration in determining support paths, and Ross's work with the parents of dyslexic students (Ross, 2019).

In discussing this dissertation project after its successful completion, Sarah described the 'snowball' effect of reading: every article gave leads to further works, and as her knowledge expanded, her sense of interest and confidence did too – culminating in an application to undertake the National Professional Qualification in Special Educational Needs Co-ordination. She experienced a sense of fulfilment in striking down subconscious notions she may have been carrying about research not being 'for her'.

Sarah also identified how much the work had actually been 'identity work'. Engaging with research has become a lot more than the simple summary and copying of other people's actions. In mapping out the landscape of research on dyslexic pupils' experience, she had clarified for herself the nature of her own experience and viewpoint, including her own knowledge parameters. She could then locate each research study in relation to that knowledge, with a clear perception of overlaps or challenges to her starting position.

In addition, she gained awareness of her own reading preferences and sticking points; she recognised the characteristics of texts which she felt drawn to read (in her case, this included texts where the writers acknowledged their own histories and viewpoints more explicitly, and quantitative studies where data on pupil experience had been collected and shared clearly and methodically). She recognised that she was more likely to dismiss or pass over texts where syntax was overly complex or expression felt abstract and academic. These insights remind us that research engagement is about more than the immediate issue at hand: it is also about the development of a nuanced understanding of your own professional identity in terms of what you use to validate your opinions and positions and what you turn away from. To know and recognise our own blind spots is to gain power in addressing them.

ACTION LEARNING SET

Imagine you have been asked to help tackle the following barrier to pupil progress in your school. It has been identified that a number of students in your age phase or subject specialism are struggling to improve their handwriting, and this is impeding the intelligibility of their responses in assessments. A quick search has yielded the following research articles.

a. Which of the following would you choose to read first and why – which might appeal to your existing reading preferences/confidence/ideas of research value?
b. Which form of data (evidence) might you expect to find most and least accessible?
c. Whom might you ask for help if the data are difficult to interpret?

A synthesis of research studies into promoting handwriting fluency carried out between 2000 and 2024 in the UK by a teacher as part of her Doctorate in Education.

A descriptive case study detailing the handwriting improvement interventions carried out in three primary schools in 1 multi-academy trust by its Research Lead.

A randomised control trial was undertaken by a team of university-based researchers assessing the efficacy of a 4-week handwriting exercise using a newly developed handwriting practice book for Year 7 pupils. Of a total of 675 pupils, 332 were randomly assigned to the handwriting exercise group.

A student voice study by an independent researcher in which 24 Year 6 pupils from 4 schools who self-identified as struggling with handwriting were asked what classroom factors helped or hindered the production of good handwriting.

What different kind of new knowledge might each of the above offer you, and how might you make use of that knowledge in your own context?

USING INSIGHTS FROM RESEARCH AS TOOLS TO HELP SOLVE PRACTICAL CLASSROOM PROBLEMS

Taking the decision to engage with research can seem challenging, but it is a great professional step forward. The practice of filtering key insights from the literature in order to turn findings into actionable steps might seem daunting, but it will bring such rewards.

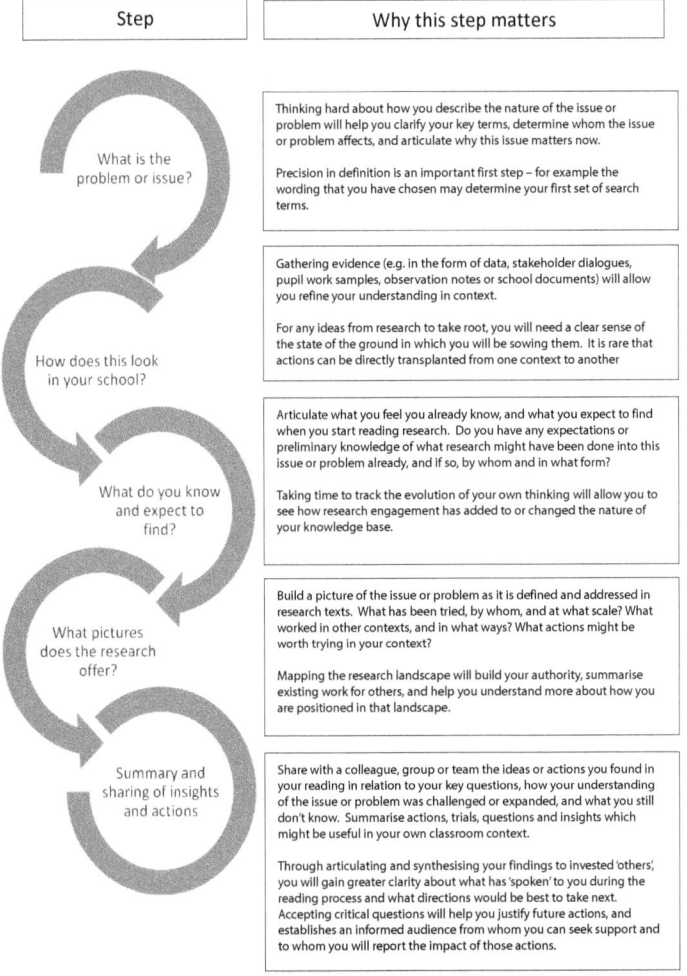

Fig. 3.1. Steps to Ensure That Practical Actions Have Been Determined Via Methodical Reasoning and Structured Foundations.

If you are striking out in a school where research engagement is not yet a fully supported aspect of school life, you might want to follow these initial steps to ensure that practical actions have been determined via methodical reasoning and structured foundations (Fig. 3.1). **Your time and energy – and that of other key stakeholders such as your pupils – is precious!**

CONCLUSION

Pearce (2022, p. xii) makes an important distinction between 'evidence informed' practice and 'evidence based' practice. She sees evidence-based practice as prescriptive in that it privileges findings from research over teachers' experiences of context. Evidence-informed practice, on the other hand, combines evidence from research with teachers' professional experience and judgement. For encounters with research to be deeply meaningful, our deep and detailed knowledge of our own classroom will always need to be brought into conversation with any findings or recommendations from research.

In keeping with Pearce's emphasis on the importance of contextual triangulation, the processes suggested in this chapter have been framed in such a way as to keep you at the centre rather than asking you to displace your contextual expertise. Research engagement should not be a rarefied activity for a privileged few but something everyone can feel confident to pursue. For schools to remain energised and sites of renewal and growth, teachers must be encouraged to continue to build themselves as learners. We would want all our pupils to be outward-looking, self-challenging, inquisitive, and well-read: this model should therefore start with us.

REVIEW OF CHAPTER OBJECTIVES

In this chapter, you have considered:

- Where research is available for teachers, and what forms research engagement might take.

- How to engage in confident and purposeful critical reading to deepen knowledge of effective classroom practice and continue your professional and personal development.

- What an impactful triangulation of theory, research and classroom practice might look like.
- How you might engage with research within school as a tool to help solve practical classroom problems.

ACKNOWLEDGEMENT

The author would like to thank Sarah Iveson for sharing aspects of her work and offering invaluable insights into teachers' experiences of engaging with engagement.

FURTHER READING AND RESOURCES

Brown, C., Flood, J., & Handscombe, G. (2020). *The research-informed teaching revolution: A handbook for the 21st century teacher.* John Catt.

Chisnell, G. (2021). *Irresistible learning: Building a culture of research in schools.* John Catt.

Firth, J. (2020). *The teacher's guide to research: Engaging with, applying and conducting research in the classroom.* Routledge.

Salles, D. (2016). *The slightly awesome teacher: Using Edu-research to get brilliant results.* John Catt.

Scott, D. (2016). *Reading educational research and policy.* Routledge.

Whitman, G. (2024). *Research-informed teaching: What it looks like in the classroom.* John Catt.

Williams, J. (2020). *How to read and understand educational research.* SAGE.

The British Educational Research Association (BERA), www.bera.ac.uk works to bring researchers and practitioners together.

Its Teacher Network is a platform to enable teachers to access and engage with research more effectively.

The National Foundation for Educational Research (NFER), www.nfer.ac.uk provides research updates and insights.

The Education Endowment Foundation (EEF), educationendowmentfoundation.org.uk is an independent charity which offers a wealth of resources to help schools and teachers engage with research, including the *Teaching and Learning Toolkit*.

REFERENCES

Amran, H. A., & Majid, R. A. (2019). Learning strategies for twice-exceptional students. *International Journal of Special Education, 33*(4), 954–976.

Burton, S. (2004). Self-esteem groups for secondary pupils with dyslexia. *Educational Psychology in Practice, 20*(1), 55–73.

Cain, T., Brindley, S., Brown, C., Jones, G., & Riga, F. (2019). Bounded decision-making, teachers' reflection and organisational learning: How research can inform teachers and teaching. *British Educational Research Journal, 45*(5), 1072–1087. https://doi.org/10.1002/berj.3551

Education Endowment Foundation. (2024). *Using research evidence: A concise guide*. https://educationendowmentfoundation.org.uk/education-evidence/more-resources-and-support/using-research-evidence

Lithari, E. (2019). Fractured academic identities: Dyslexia, secondary education, self-esteem and school experiences. *International Journal of Inclusive Education, 23*(3), 280–296.

Pearce, J. (2022). *What every teacher needs to know: How to embed evidence-informed teaching and learning in your school*. Bloomsbury Education.

Proctor, R. (2013). Teachers and research: What they value and what they do. *Journal of Pedagogic Development, 3*(1). https://www.beds.ac.uk/jpd/volume-3-issue-1/teachers-and-research-what-they-value-and-what-they-do

Ross, H. (2019). Supporting a child with dyslexia: How parents/carers engage with school-based support for their children. *British Journal of Special Education, 46*(2), 136–156.

Rowan, L. (2010). Learning with dyslexia in secondary school in New Zealand: What can we learn from students' past experiences? *Australian Journal of Learning Difficulties, 15*(1), 71–79.

4

USING RESEARCH FOR ADAPTIVE TEACHING: RESPONDING TO ALL LEARNERS

Evan McCormick

Leeds Trinity University, UK

CHAPTER OBJECTIVES

In this chapter, you will:

- Consider what adaptive teaching is and its importance in creating an inclusive learning environment.
- Explore why teachers' knowledge of individual learners, at the 'micro-level', is needed for adaptive teaching.
- Examine how collaborating with all in the school community, at the 'meso-level', can contribute to adaptive teaching practices.
- Consider the potential impact of 'macro-level' educational research on adaptive teaching strategies.

Keywords: Adaptive teaching; scaffolding; high expectations; differentiation; special educational needs and disabilities (SEND); English as an additional language (EAL)

INTRODUCTION

You might have heard that teachers 'have eyes in the back of their heads'. While the saying is unfortunately not literally true, it does highlight the demanding nature of the work teachers do. To navigate such demands, successful teachers employ a range of *adaptive* strategies to *respond* to learners' needs. This chapter uses evidence from research to develop a deeper understanding of and build teachers' confidence in *adaptive teaching*, focussing on ensuring strategies you adopt are aligned to your specific context and learners' needs. Adaptive teaching, the fifth domain of the Initial Teacher Training and Early Career Framework (ITTECF) (Department for Education, 2024), can offer more inclusive and supportive learning environments when implemented effectively.

This chapter will begin by defining adaptive teaching and outlining who it is intended for. It will support you, as a research-informed practitioner, to critically consider the approaches available to you. This requires an understanding of learners' needs, especially those with special educational needs and disabilities (SEND) or English as an additional language (EAL). Like other chapters in this book, a broad approach to what constitutes 'research' is taken – comprising both existing research and your evidence finding in school. In this chapter, I propose a model of three interdependent research knowledge bases: the micro-level (understanding individual learners and your own classroom practice), the meso-level (engaging with your school community), and the macro-level (using wider educational research). I conclude with a case study demonstrating how a successful school utilises all three of these knowledge bases.

WHAT IS ADAPTIVE TEACHING?

The term '*adaptive teaching*' has gained considerable traction in recent years, resulting in a shift in how classroom pedagogy is understood and conceptualised. Central to the ITTECF (Department for Education, 2024), it is not only crucial for trainees and early career teachers (ECTs) to understand the importance of adaptive teaching, but also to gain confidence in deploying a range of adaptive teaching strategies.

The concept of adaptive teaching can be understood through three central principles.

The Teacher Being Actively Engaged

The ITTECF (Department for Education, 2024) provides us with some unambiguous and useful expectations around adaptive teaching, emphasising the necessity to be 'responsive', provide 'targeted support', and 'understand pupils' differences' (p. 20). From this, it is evident adaptive teaching requires teachers to be actively engaged, sustaining their ongoing presence in the classroom, responding to learners' 'understanding, progress, and (learnt) motivation' to enhance learning (Knapton, 2022, p. 7). Adaptive teaching is a didactic, learner-centred exchange, rather than a teacher-centred approach.

The Teacher Being Responsive to Individual Learners' Needs

We can now begin to consider what is involved in this learner-centred interaction. For Schipper et al. (2018), teachers should respond and adapt through 'adjustments of their planning and teaching to meet the individual educational needs' (p. 110), while for Gallagher et al. (2022), adaptive teaching is the 'teacher's unplanned response' (p. 299). Reflecting on these two definitions, the complexity of the task at hand becomes clear: meeting the diverse needs of up to 30 learners in a single classroom sounds, and can sometimes be, overwhelming. However, pupils and students have always had their individual needs – a framework for identifying and responding to those needs is offered through adaptive teaching, something previous pedagogical approaches, namely differentiation, often did not fully achieve.

The Teacher Having High Expectations For All

The ITTECF (Department for Education, 2024) highlights that all educators need to have *high expectations* for all learners, and it characterises successful teachers as being 'key role models' who can and do 'affect pupil outcomes' (p. 11). In summary, positive relationships and the expectations teachers set have a lasting impact on attainment. For Gallagher et al. (2022), adaptive teaching supports everyone's 'needs while holding high expectations for their learning' (p. 299). In practice, adaptive teaching involves all learners working towards a common set of learning goals. Teachers then provide focussed support, like scaffolding or adult support, to individuals or small groups who require it. To deliver effectively, teachers need an in-depth knowledge of all learners in their class. While we may of course expect individuals' outcomes and confidence in learning to differ according to their own skills and knowledge bases, this approach does not put a ceiling on expectations, seeing no reason for a learner not to work towards the same learning out-come as others. High expectations from adaptive teaching can contribute to a culture of motivation and self-efficacy and ensure equity in opportunity for pupils and students with SEND and EAL.

ADAPTIVE TEACHING VERSUS DIFFERENTIATION

Adaptive teaching has gained prominence over differentiation in recent years. Confusingly, the terms are sometimes used interchangeably both in schools and in educational research. Knapton (2022) notes that while adaptive teaching could be interpreted as a rebranding of differentiation, it represents 'a more fundamental shift' in pedagogical approach (p. 9). Griffiths (2024) also identifies 'significant differences', with differentiation often delivered through the creation and completion of a range of levelled tasks, instead of requiring teachers to respond to individuals' needs as they emerge (p. 189).

We will now consider the difference between adaptive teaching and differentiation in some more detail. To do this, we will reframe the three central principles of adaptive teaching, instead considering them against differentiation.

The Teacher May Not Be Actively Engaged

If differentiation requires producing multiple pre-planned, levelled tasks, a demand exists on teachers' time and energy away from the classroom. Eaton (2022), writing for the Educational Endowment Foundation (EEF), links this to 'an accountability system' that encouraged teachers to demonstrate differentiation by creating multiple worksheets (para. 1). Ikwumelu et al. (2015) add that this discourages innovation and can make teachers resistant to adaptive practices. In effect, teachers' capacity and need to adapt dynamically during lessons can be reduced by rigid, levelled, pre-planned tasks.

The Teacher May Not Be Responsive To Individual Learners' Needs

Differentiation practices typically use static ability grouping, setting tasks based on perceived ability. When the perceived ability of the learner is the gauge for the activity being set, the task may then not offer adequate challenge to all. Individuals may face a challenge in a levelled task, but what if the task is not challenging enough? Without sufficient challenge, opportunities for the teacher to dynamically support learning may be diminished. This may restrict the teacher's need to adapt teaching strategies to address individual learners' progress, emerging misconceptions, or changes in their motivation.

The Teacher May Not Have High Expectations For All

A significant criticism of differentiation lies in its potential to impose a ceiling upon learning. Eaton (2022) highlights this issue by providing the example of 'the bottom group' receiving 'a different task to everyone else', regardless of their ability in that particular area of learning. This raises concerns around equity and inclusion, undermining learners' self-efficacy and motivation for learning.

ADAPTIVE TEACHING IN PRACTICE

As adaptive teaching removes the need to view pupils and students in fixed ability categories, it creates space to consider individual need and to group learners flexibly. This aligns with ITTECF (Department for Education, 2024), which emphasises the requirement for teachers to use flexible grouping to 'provide more tailored support' (p. 20).

In a single day, across several subjects, individuals may work in various groupings with a variety of peers, highlighting how each learner brings their own individual strengths and areas for growth to the classroom. At this point, you may be considering how pupils and students with SEND fit into this picture. The ITTECF (Department for Education, 2024) highlights that those with SEND are 'likely to require additional or adapted support' (p. 21), a statutory requirement otherwise enshrined in the SEND Code of Practice (Department for Education & Department of Health, 2015). The ITTECF (Department for Education, 2024) additionally reminds us that all learners 'are likely to learn at different rates and require varying levels of support to succeed' (p. 20). Adaptive teaching therefore moves away from framing pupils and students with SEND as having the 'most need'. In some cases, these learners may demonstrate greater confidence in certain learning objectives compared to their peers without such a label. Indeed, at other times, learners with SEND may in fact require additional support.

This also applies to pupils and students with EAL. As Mistry and Sood (2020) highlight, EAL is an 'umbrella term' for children with a 'range of different language competencies' (p. 76), whose confidence can vary depending on the subject or task at hand. EAL learners are not a homogenous group and, therefore, a lack of proficiency should never be assumed. In my own career, I have taught learners who were officially classified as EAL yet have been exposed to English throughout their lives. For other learners, as I knew they had an extensive understanding of complex concepts in their first language, making appropriate adaptations allowed them to excel. As a flexible approach, adaptive teaching can therefore accommodate the 'natural diversity' of the classroom, including learners with SEND and EAL. It does not need to reduce educational rigour for any group (Borich, 2017, p. 37) and can ensure equitable opportunities for all (Vaughn et al., 2022).

EXAMPLES OF ADAPTIVE TEACHING STRATEGIES

These strategies are adapted from Griffiths (2024), Mosey and Stothard (2024) and Westwood (2024). Divided into 'Remediation' and 'Compensatory' approaches, as suggested by Borich (2017, p. 37), this classification provides an additional lens for evaluating when and why adaptive teaching strategies should be used (see Table 4.1).

THREE RESEARCH KNOWLEDGE BASES FOR ADAPTIVE TEACHING

We will now consider how you use your own research to implement adaptive teaching. In 2014, the British Education Research Association (BERA) published a report into the role of research in education, titled 'Research and the Teaching Profession', which called on teachers to engage in both 'enquiry-based practice' and develop a 'research-rich culture' in schools (p. 37). While the role of research in our schools has developed over the past decade, I highlight this report as these key messages form the basis of the 'Three Research Knowledge Bases for Adaptive Teaching' I propose.

Schools are undeniably evidence-rich places, from quantitative data gathered in summative assessments to qualitative data gathered during discussions with colleagues. Teachers are well-used to information gathering and, from this, coming up with all sorts of creative solutions using both quantitative and qualitative data. Nevertheless, however well-intended these solutions may be, a research-informed lens is needed to ensure they are impactful. Without a grounding in credible research, a risk of misusing evidence exists, which may lead to adopting strategies that do not benefit all learners (see Chapter 4 for more information on this). When developing approaches to adaptive teaching, I encourage you to rely upon each of the three knowledge bases below (see Fig. 4.1), recognising them as inter-reliant within a cyclical process, informing and supporting each other.

THE MICRO-LEVEL: UNDERSTANDING INDIVIDUAL LEARNERS AND YOUR OWN CLASSROOM PRACTICE

As we have already learned by introducing the research evidence, an adaptive teacher uses precise knowledge of learners in the

Table 4.1. Strategies for Adaptive Teaching.

Strategy	Description	Example
The **remediation approach** requires direct action before or after whole-class teaching. It aims to provide knowledge, skills, or behaviours needed to engage with or retain learning		
Pre-teach	Teaching key concepts to specific learners before a lesson	Reviewing shape vocabulary with Year 2 pupils with EAL before a lesson on geometry
Post-teach	Reinforcing learning after a lesson to secure this	Repeating a long division question with Year 6 pupils
Home learning	Assigning specific home learning to consolidate knowledge	Giving a small group of Reception pupils phonics cards to practice blending at home
The **compensatory approach** may also be planned ahead, but is instead delivered during teaching by modifying content, delivery, or resources		
Adjusting depth or complexity	Adapting the level of challenge to suit individual learner needs	A Year 4 times tables lesson where pupils work on a range of multiples
Omitting or adding content	Tailoring lesson content to focus on essential or additional elements	Assessing a Year 5 child's science knowledge by voice recording, instead of writing
Instruction and questioning	Modifying the way questions are asked or instructions are given	In a Year 6 history lesson, asking a pupil a leading literal question, followed by an open question
Scaffolding with resources	Providing physical or visual aids to reduce cognitive load	Some pupils use a rekenrek and others use a number line in Year 1 Maths

Source: Informed by Borich (2017), Griffiths (2024), Mosey & Stothard (2024) and Westwood (2024).

classroom to identify approaches to support learning. This, coupled with an understanding of your own strengths and preferences as a teacher, forms the first research knowledge base. The commonly used analogy of teaching being like cooking a meal, with diners having differing tastes and dietary needs, is helpful in outlining the need for this knowledge base. To make the meal enjoyable and nourishing, you need to consider your diners (*your learners*), the ingredients you have (*your resources*), and your skillset as a cook (*your strengths*). Reflection on this allows you to adjust flavours and ingredients, serving a meal that suits all. Some plates may take more effort than others, yet the majority will be served the same. Here, we can start to see why any adoption of pre-prepared and commercially published schemes of learning must be carefully considered and adapted, with the scheme being like a recipe from a book: it will provide a foundation, but it does not account for who is at the table. A successful meal takes research and effort beforehand and may require additional changes while being served.

The analogy highlights how teaching requires responsiveness to individuals' needs and begins to suggest how the teacher is an informal 'action researcher'. Chapter 6 provides further information on developing action research within your school. As Mosey and Stothard (2024) point out, through formative assessment, teachers engage in 'ongoing and continuous' data collection (p. 12), with the purpose of using this data diagnostically 'to adapt learning and teaching' (p. 13). To Bradbury et al. (2019), this diagnostic element is central to action research, which addresses a 'continuous need' to make classroom practices 'better' (p. 7). Day-to-day adaptive teaching is like continually completing action research: it is diagnostic in its aims, moving from identifying individual learners' needs and barriers to making informed decisions about how to adjust teaching.

Action Research in Practice

A further way we can see the adaptive teacher acting as a researcher is action research's close alignment with The Graduated Approach (Department for Education & Department of Health, 2015). While

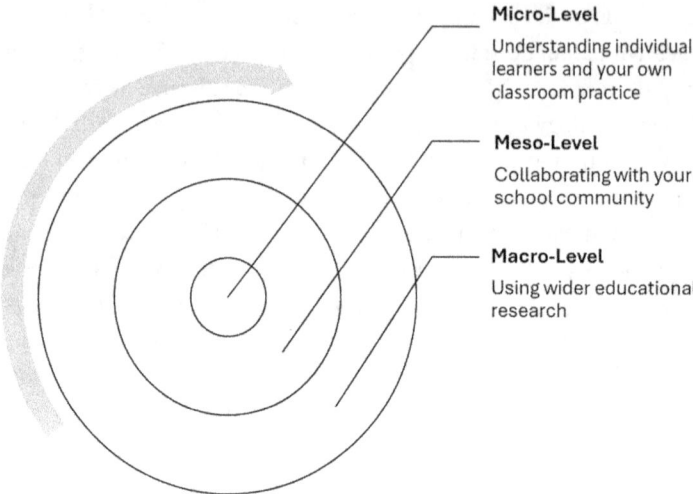

Fig. 4.1. The Three Research Knowledge Bases for Adaptive Teaching.

intended as a structured approach for planning provision for pupils and students with SEND, the framework provides a practical model for adaptive teaching more broadly (Cowne et al., 2018). Its emphasis on targeted assessment and ongoing evaluation offers you a methodology for identifying specific barriers to learning and, importantly, implementing precise and timely adaptive measures (see Fig. 4.2).

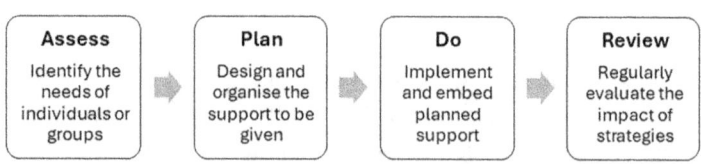

Fig. 4.2. The 'Graduate Approach Method' Informed by Department for Education and Department of Health (2015).

It is important to recognise that true action research requires elements that may make teachers feel uneasy, namely, the inclusion of educational theory and the dissemination of results. As Taylor (2017) points out, teachers often do not see themselves as researchers for these reasons (see Chapter 4 for further details on engaging with research evidence and educational theory). Stringer (2019) identifies that educational theory is an essential aspect of action

> **REFLECTIVE QUESTIONS**
>
> Recalling your experiences of adaptive teaching, begin to relate these to The Graduated Approach model above.
>
> - How do you currently *assess* pupils' needs to inform your adaptive teaching?
> - How do you *plan* to support based on assessments?
> - How do you *implement* these adaptations in practice? Do you adjust these as you teach?
> - How do you *review* the impact? What evidence informs this process?

research; fear of it should not be a deterrent. While they may not be conscious of it, successful adaptive teachers engage with educational theory by drawing on research-based strategies, such as scaffolding, to address learners' needs'. Similarly, they disseminate results when writing Individual Education Plans and by collaborating with colleagues to share effective practices and outcomes.

THE MESO-LEVEL: ENGAGING WITH YOUR SCHOOL COMMUNITY

Adaptive teachers must be skilled in collaborating other stakeholders and, crucially, recognising when to seek support. As our 'meso-level' knowledge base, this principle is embedded within the ITTECF (Department for Education, 2024) itself, which highlights the need for adaptive teachers to work 'closely' with the Special Educational Needs Coordinator (SENDCo), other experts, the Designated Safeguarding Lead (DSL), and, importantly, parents (p. 20). Creating shared goals among all staff and with parents is essential for the pupil or student. It is important these relationships are reciprocal: adaptive teachers might gain information from Teaching Assistants (TAs) and parents about specific learners to inform their approaches but should also share their expertise on what works for learners. Similarly, SENCOs and other experts bring specialist knowledge and should be viewed as a vital source for advising on adaptive practices. They may offer specific strategies, model these approaches, and support you in their implementation.

While working with confident and experienced TAs can be intimidating for both new and experienced teachers, it is important to recognise how they can become a key adaptive resource. Support staff need to feel valued, working to recognise their individual skill sets so that they are deployed effectively. This requires careful consideration: the Education Endowment Foundation (2021) warns that the teacher retains primary responsibility for learning when deploying TAs. This means ensuring proper guidance and direction. An example of effective direction may be requesting your TA to work with a small group of pupils during a Year 4 Maths lesson. After giving an initial instruction to work with the pupils on the whole-class learning objective, further advice focuses on the specific area they need support with, based upon your earlier formative assessments.

You may have had times when you have felt inferior due to having less experience, particularly as a trainee or ECT. However, as Mosey and Stothard (2024) point out, having recently engaged in teacher training and being aware of current educational practices places you in a strong position to support colleagues. A similar experience is shared by experienced teachers who move to a new school environment. In both situations, not only will school senior leaders hope you to settle in well, but they will also want you to enrich the school community by sharing your knowledge of good practice and approaches to adaptive teaching. This is an expectation of the ITTECF (Department for Education, 2024), which outlines how teachers should contribute to school development. You should openly share your approaches to adaptive teaching with your colleagues. Even better, developing opportunities to collaborate using the Graduated Approach to devise new strategies could offer a valuable opportunity for shared professional development. Lambirth et al. (2019) highlight how such collaboration can lead teachers to exchange and formulate creative solutions, which will in turn enrich your adaptive teaching approaches. So, capitalise on your professional relationships with colleagues from early in your career; exchanging strategies and learning from each other's successes can improve your practice and outcomes for children.

> **REFLECTIVE QUESTIONS**
>
> - How regularly do you exchange insights with parents on learners' needs?
> - How do you guide and support TAs to effectively contribute to adaptive teaching?
> - How can you use professional relationships and collaboration to further develop your approaches to adaptive teaching?

THE MACRO-LEVEL: USING WIDER EDUCATIONAL RESEARCH

As a research-informed 'adaptive' practitioner, combining your professional expertise with dependable research is a key objective. When engaging with 'macro-level' broader educational research, the third knowledge base, adaptive teaching, emphasises the need for 'research thinking'. Willison (2024) describes this as a form of thinking that 'prioritises teacher professional judgment which heeds research' (p. 3). In essence, it is a two-way exchange: the 'informed' opinion holds value, yet the 'information' becomes meaningless without an understanding of the individual learner.

Chapter 4 of this book usefully leads you through the process of identifying relevant literary research to support your learning and practice. As a starting point in looking for credible research, subject- and age-specific magazines are often useful. For example, Teaching English by NATE often publishes small-scale yet informative studies and spotlights wider trends. The EEF and DfE websites are also useful, as well as peer-reviewed journals like the British Educational Research Journal, where many articles are open access. With the adaptive teaching strategies you identify from these sources, it is important to consider whether they meet the needs of the children in your classroom. Below is a specific example of how wider educational research can be used to inform your adaptive teaching knowledge and understanding.

Using Wider Educational Research to Inform Practice

It's the start of the Spring term, and Mark, an experienced Reception teacher, is reviewing the progress of his class. A group of six pupils are not yet on track to meet the Communication and Language Early Learning Goals (ELGs). While this trend had been identified in September's baseline assessment, Mark initially hoped these children would progress naturally through adult- and peer-interactions. Therefore, no specific strategies had been put in place. Now, without the staffing to run a specific intervention programme, Mark needs to use an in-class adaptive teaching strategy. After seeing a suggestion on social media about effective storytelling, Mark researches the relevant area of the EEF website. He finds evidence that one-to-one 'interactive reading' can boost vocabulary and comprehension. So, to support these pupils, Mark begins reading whole-class picture books with this group on a one-to-one basis, before sharing the story as a whole class. During this one-to-one active read, Mark encourages them to take the lead in speaking about what they notice in the pictures, as he reads the text. After several weeks, Mark notices significant improvements in their vocabulary and confidence in describing the books. The positive impact is then confirmed through language assessments.

> **CASE STUDY**
>
> The following interview is provided by a SENCo at a three-form primary school serving a diverse community. It illustrates how the school applies the Three Knowledge Bases for Adaptive Teaching to meet children's needs and support their learning.
>
> As you read the interview, consider how the school:
>
> - Identifies and responds to learners' needs.
> - Balances professional judgement with research evidence.
> - Adapts teaching to reflect the diversity of learners.
> - Uses collaboration among staff to share expertise.

What Is the School's Approach to Adaptive Teaching?

Our school's approach to adaptive teaching is very much about understanding the individual child. Our children come from a wide range of different backgrounds, and that means they bring different needs to the classroom. So, it's important as you're teaching them to understand that not every approach is going to work. As the SENCo for the school, I'm always trying to encourage our teachers to make small, meaningful adjustments to their teaching. It might be through grouping differently, using different forms of scaffolding, and we also find that visuals work for a lot of our children too. We also value teachers' expertise and trust them to make decisions for themselves. We do have various whole-school strategies that we encourage teachers to adopt, but if they have a strategy that works for them, then we are more than happy for them to use it. Our whole-school strategies are evidence-based; they come from various sources like EEF guidance and education research journals, and that's important so that we're able to share with our staff, governors, and parents a deep understanding of how our teaching and learning works.

How Do You Know Pupils' Needs Are Met? What About Pupils With SEND or EAL?

Our teachers know how to deal with problems quickly as they arise. Also, each year group has a prescribed structure for regular assessments through different means, and we meet with our teachers termly to discuss progress and receive the more qualitative information on why certain children aren't making progress. We collaborate with our parents to create support plans for SEND and EAL learners too. We're lucky to have support from educational psychologists, speech and language therapists, and play therapists, and that all feeds into support plans. Some of our SEND and EAL pupils do receive targeted support through interventions. However, most of their needs are met within the classroom, and that's because we've got a strong vision for adaptive teaching in place.

How Are TAs Deployed at Your School?

This is an impossible question to answer because no two TAs in our school have the same job role. Some of them might deliver interventions during the day, offer small group support, or act as the teacher while the teacher works with a small group. There are lots of different ways our TAs are deployed. We recognise that they are a key resource for us in adaptive teaching, and we really value their flexibility and knowledge base. They're often the first responders to children, so we include them in discussions on children's progress too.

How Are ECTs Supported in Developing Their Adaptive Teaching Practice?

We're lucky to have four ECTs this year. Of course, they're paired with an experienced mentor, and they engage in CPD. Some of this will be focussed on adaptive teaching practice. Something additional that all teachers do at our school is lesson study, where groups of three work together to trial strategies, reflect, and share with peers. We then have a staff conference where everyone shares their ideas, and this is how many of adaptive teaching strategies used in our school are disseminated. It's an effective and supportive way to share good practice.

Can You Tell Us About One of the Whole-school Approaches to Adaptive Teaching? How Did This Come About?

Something that comes to mind is our use of sign language in Early Years and Key Stage One. This was led by one of our

ECTs teaching Year 1, who had some basic knowledge of sign language and started to implement it when asking key instructions. It was really clear the impact this was having for all children in their language development, but particularly EAL and SEND learners. The ECT did some wider research on it and presented it in a staff meeting. Now all staff from Nursery to Year 2 use some key pieces of sign language after we invested in training. You can see that this is an adaptive approach that is targeted towards certain children, but all children benefit. The children don't notice the difference.

Have There Been Any Adaptive Teaching Practices That Haven't Worked?

Well, of course, our practice is always developing and doesn't stay the same. That's the whole purpose of engaging in the lesson study, for example. The key change is the idea of differentiating work and having different tasks for abilities – I don't even like that word now. We once thought that was effective, but we've since directed our practice away from that.

In summary, using the Three Research Knowledge Bases can ensure that adaptive teaching is based upon:

- A robust evidence base, whether through school data or wider educational research.
- Purposeful collaboration with colleagues and professionals.
- A cycle of reflection and improvement, which particularly supports trainees and ECTs.

CONCLUSION

In this chapter, you have explored how research-informed adaptive teaching can create inclusive learning environments and meet learners' needs. I have introduced a model of three interdependent research knowledge bases: the micro-level, the meso-level, and the macro-level. By engaging with these knowledge bases, teachers can develop effective, context-specific approaches to adaptive teaching. The chapter has highlighted the value of your expertise and has encouraged you to take a proactive role in seeking solutions, including through engaging with an action research cycle.

> **REVIEW OF CHAPTER OBJECTIVES**
>
> In this chapter, you have:
>
> - Considered what adaptive teaching is and its importance in creating an inclusive learning environment.
> - Explored why teachers' knowledge of individual learners, at the 'micro-level', is needed for adaptive teaching.
> - Examined how collaborating with all in the school community, at the 'meso-level', can contribute to adaptive teaching practices.
> - Considered the potential impact of 'macro-level' educational research on adaptive teaching strategies.

FURTHER READING AND RESOURCES

Education Endowment Foundation. (2021). *Special educational needs in mainstream schools [Guidance report]*. EEF. Retrieved January 4, 2025, from https://educationendowmentfoundation.org.uk/education-evidence/guidance-reports/send

Mosey, C., & Stothard, J. (2024). *Adaptive teaching in primary schools: A toolkit for trainee teachers*. Learning Matters.

Westwood, P. S. (2024). *Inclusive and adaptive teaching: Meeting the challenge of diversity in the classroom* (3rd ed.). David Fulton Publishers.

REFERENCES

Borich, G. D. (2017). *Effective teaching methods: Research-based practice* (9th ed.). Pearson Publishers.

Bradbury, H., Lewis, R., & Embury, D. C. (2019). Education action research: With and for the next generation. In C. A. Metler (Ed.), *The Wiley handbook of action research in education* (pp. 5–28). Wiley.

British Educational Research Association. (2014). *Research and the teaching profession: Building the capacity for a self-improving education system [report]*. British Educational Research Association. Retrieved January 2, 2025, from https://www.bera.ac.uk/wp-content/uploads/2013/12/BERA-RSA-Research-Teaching-Profession-FULL-REPORT-for-web.pdf

Cowne, E., Frankl, C., & Gerschel, L. (2018). *The SENCo handbook: Leading and managing a whole school approach*. Routledge.

Department for Education & Department of Health. (2015). *Special educational needs and disability code of practice: 0 to 25 years*. Department for Education & Department of Health. Retrieved January 2, 2025, from https://assets.publishing.service.gov.uk/media/5a7dcb85ed915d2ac884d995/SEND_Code_of_Practice_January_2015.pdf

Department for Education. (2024). *Initial teacher training and early career framework*. Department for Education. Retrieved January 2, 2025, from https://assets.publishing.service.gov.uk/media/661d24ac08c3be25cfbd3e61/Initial_Teacher_Training_and_Early_Career_Framework.pdf

Eaton, J. (2022, October 19). Moving from 'differentiation' to 'adaptive teaching'. *EEF Blog*. Retrieved January 2, 2025, from https://educationendowmentfoundation.org.uk/news/moving-from-differentiation-to-adaptive-teaching

Education Endowment Foundation. (2021). *Making best use of teaching assistants [guidance report]*. EEF. Retrieved January 4, 2025, from https://educationendowmentfoundation.org.uk/education-evidence/guidance-reports/send

Gallagher, M. A., Parsons, S. A., & Vaughn, M. (2022). Adaptive teaching in mathematics: A review of the literature. *Educational Review*, 74(2), 298–320. https://doi.org/10.1080/00131911.2020.1722065

Griffiths, A. (2024). Adaptive teaching. In M. Stephenson & A. Gill (Eds.), *Training to be a primary school teacher: ITT and beyond* (pp. 185–202). Learning Matters.

Ikwumelu, S. N., Oyibe, O. A., & Oketa, E. C. (2015). Adaptive teaching: An invaluable pedagogic practice in social studies education. *Journal of Education and Practice*, 6(33), 140–144. https://eric.ed.gov/?id=EJ1083517

Knapton, H. (2022). Differentiation vs adaptive teaching? *Teaching Business & Economics*, 26(1), 7–9. https://www.proquest.com/scholarly-journals/differentiation-vs-adaptive-teaching/docview/2852979421/se-2?accountid=11979

Lambirth, A., Cabral, A., McDonald, R., Philpott, C., Brett, A., & Magaji, A. (2019). Teacher-led professional development through a model of action research, collaboration and facilitation. *Professional Development in Education*, 47(5), 815–833. https://doi.org/10.1080/19415257.2019.1685565

Mistry, M., & Sood, K. (2020). *Meeting the needs of young children with English as an additional language: Research informed practice*. Routledge.

Mosey, C., & Stothard, J. (2024). *Adaptive teaching in primary schools: A toolkit for trainee teachers*. Learning Matters.

Schipper, T., Goei, S. L., de Vries, S., & van Veen, K. (2018). Developing teachers' self-efficacy and adaptive teaching behaviour through lesson study. *International Journal of Educational Research*, 88, 109–120. https://doi.org/10.1016/j.ijer.2018.01.011

Stringer, E. (2019). Theory in educational action research. In C. A. Metler (Ed.), *The Wiley handbook of action research in education* (pp. 139–160). Wiley.

Taylor, L. A. (2017). How teachers become teacher researchers: Narrative as a tool for teacher identity construction. *Teaching and Teacher Education*, 61, 16–25.

Vaughn, M., Parsons, S. A., & Gallagher, M. A. (2022). Challenging scripted curricula with adaptive teaching. *Educational Researcher*, *51*(3), 186–196. https://doi.org/10.3102/0013189X211065752

Westwood, P. S. (2024). *Inclusive and adaptive teaching: Meeting the challenge of diversity in the classroom* (3rd ed.). David Fulton Publishers.

Willison, J. (2024). Teachers' research thinking. In J. Willison (Ed.), *Research thinking for responsive teaching: Research skill development with in-service and preservice educators* (pp. 1–14). Springer.

5

BEING AN ETHICAL PRACTITIONER RESEARCHER: CONDUCTING YOUR OWN RESEARCH AND APPLYING RESEARCH ETHICALLY

Aimee Quickfall

Leeds Trinity University, UK

CHAPTER OBJECTIVES

In this chapter, you will:

- Find an introduction to the basic aspects of research ethics and the importance of ethical practices when carrying out and applying research.
- Explore how research can be carried out ethically in the classroom and with children.
- Reflect on the importance of self-care for researchers.

Keywords: Anonymity; consent; data storage and management; ethics; ethical approval; harm

INTRODUCTION

This chapter introduces the reader to research ethics, both from a legal and formal perspective and in terms of being mindful of how research is carried out ethically and, importantly, *used ethically* in the classroom. From carrying out your first piece of research to applying research literature to your own setting, ethics should be central to your decision-making.

The chapter will also cover self-care for researchers with a focus on practitioner research, with practical advice, guidance and sources of support for practitioner researchers on how to ensure their work is ethical.

A case study will be shared of practitioner experience in both carrying out research in terms of ethics, including some examples of where unexpected situations can present ethical dilemmas, and how to tackle challenges before and when they arise.

ETHICAL PRINCIPLES FOR EDUCATIONAL RESEARCH

Research ethics, very simply, are moral principles that guide how researchers should conduct their work. Thinking about research ethics can take over your life, particularly if you are undertaking research yourself. As a researcher I have had sleepless nights over ethical dilemmas, and in this chapter I hope to help you avoid those, but at the same time, reassure you that if you do have ethical challenges and concerns, this is normal and there are practical steps you can take both in the early design stages of a project, and during the research to alleviate those concerns. In fact, it has been argued that ethical issues are an 'important element of researcher development and identity' (Head, 2020, p. 73).

Research ethics are a vital aspect of designing and undertaking research. Maintaining ethical principles such as informed consent, anonymity, data protection, and consideration of participants means that research can happen without causing harm or distress, and that findings from the research can be used to further the understanding in the field. Educational researchers work to understand the wide and varied discipline of education, and are themselves a varied group; researchers may be working in schools and settings, in universities and research institutes, they may be students on education programmes such as initial teacher education (ITE), and they may also be independent researchers. In education, the British Educational Research Association (2024) (BERA) guidelines are a set of guidelines used by researchers in the discipline and are informative and helpful; other ethics guidelines are also available for other disciplines, such as psychology (British Psychological Society, 2021) and sociology (British Psychological Society, 2017), as well as social research more generally (Social Research Association, 2021). The British Educational Research Association (2024) guidelines set out how research should be conducted with respect, care and trust for 'people; knowledge; the quality of educational research; the environment; and academic freedom' (British Educational Research Association, 2024, para. 2).

Depending on whether you are a student teacher, student researcher, teacher, or independent researcher will make a difference to how you approach ethics from a legal and procedural standpoint. For example, if you are a student or working in higher education, each university has its own ethics protocols, supplemented by discipline-specific guidance and overseen and upheld by an ethics review board (ERB) or panel. These processes have been enacted to protect participants from exploitative research, addressing many notorious examples of unethical research, and to protect universities from reputational and legal damage (Busher & Fox, 2021). However, the importance of taking an ethical stance is much more than avoiding lawsuits – as Mauthner et al. (2012) point out, if we are not ethical as researchers, we will 'be letting others down who we made a pact with – our participants who "gifted" their words to us, and the readers of our findings' (Mauthner et al., 2012, p. 180). Here, the advice given is based on the BERA guidelines, including the case study resolution later in this chapter.

If you are working in a school or education setting, your employing setting may have ethical guidelines or processes for you to follow if you want to undertake your own research, which you must follow; if in any doubt, seek advice from your own institution/employer.

Whatever your current situation and position, it is important to consider research ethics, not only when conducting research with children and others, but also when we are considering research findings produced by others and applying those to our own work. You can read more about understanding how to use certain types of research in Chapters 2 and 4. It is also of vital importance that, as producers and consumers of research, we ensure we ourselves are supported and protected – this is an important aspect of ethics. It is also important that we do not consider the gaining of formal ethical approval from an institution as the end of our ethical thinking when doing and using research (Miller & Bell, 2012; Quickfall, 2022).

RESEARCHING ETHICALLY

In this section, we will consider some of the main ethical considerations for educational researchers, and you can find more information about this in the British Educational Research Association (2024) guidelines, as well as through your institution if appropriate and in the further reading at the end of the chapter.

Responsibilities to Participants

As a researcher, you have a responsibility to your participants. This covers fundamental issues such as doing no harm to them, but also more nuanced issues like avoiding the collection of unnecessary data, which is a waste of time and effort for your participants (and you!). Researchers must treat participants with respect, and without prejudice; research based on discriminatory assumptions, or treating participants unfairly would certainly not be ethical. Researchers should also be aware of inequalities in their own relationships with participants, and the power and pressure researchers can exert. In classroom based research for example, children and staff may feel obliged to take part in research and it may be difficult for them to say no, or to withdraw from a research project once they have started.

Interestingly, the United Nations Convention on the Rights of the Child (UNCRC) sets out the rights of children to express views on matters that impact them, including participation in research.

If you are working with participants who are children, part of your responsibility as a researcher is to make sure that, as far as possible, children understand what is happening, have the opportunity to voice an opinion on their participation, and have this view respected. For example, a practical action to help with this is producing information sheets and consent forms for children that are designed for them (see the case study for a real-life example of this).

Consent and Right to Withdraw

Consent should be sought from participants in advance of the research project beginning, and this should be informed consent in almost all cases, meaning that participants understand what the research project is aiming to do, the methods that will be used and where their data will be used. Even though consent has been given at the beginning of the research, researchers should be aware that participants may change their minds, and particularly when working with vulnerable participants (such as children), should regularly check in with participants to ensure they are happy to continue taking part. The same applies to non-vulnerable participants. Participants should also be informed about how to withdraw their data from the project, if they change their mind about participation; they should be told who to contact and the deadline for withdrawing their data. As the researcher, it is then your job to find and delete the data, so you must carefully consider in advance if this is possible, for example, if the participant has been part of a focus group of many participants, where taking out one person in the conversation would not make sense. Researchers may approach parents for consent and forget that child participants should also be given the opportunity to choose whether they want to take part. If the researcher is aware of the power and influence they may bring to the researcher/participant relationship, they are in a better position to mitigate against this. For example, the researcher may ask another member of staff to introduce the project and ask children if they would like to take part, stressing that they do not have to.

Privacy and Data Storage

It is important that the privacy and dignity of participants are protected, and hence, researchers ordinarily will anonymise their data before publication or sharing with any audience. This may mean changing the names of participants for a pseudonym, but also may require changes to the name of a school, town, other people who are mentioned in the data, and also needs careful consideration if the participant could be identified from things they have described or reported. For example, a participant who has a complex set of needs, an unusual set of demographic data (age, gender, ethnicity, religion etc.), plus a particular way of expressing themselves, may be very easily identified by someone who knows them, if participant quotes are used in conjunction with a summary of the participant's information and demographic data. Data, once collected, must also be carefully managed and stored to ensure it is secure. Participants should be made aware before they participate about how their data will be collected, stored and anonymised, who it will be shared with, how long the data will be kept and how it will be used (e.g., for publication in a book).

Incentives

Some research projects offer participants incentives for taking part, and it is really important that, as researchers, we consider what is proportionate as an incentive and what is appropriate to offer. Too generous an incentive can make it difficult for prospective participants to reject, even if they have concerns about the study, and some incentives are not appropriate. When working with children, it is important that incentives are proportionate, fair and agreed with key stakeholders, such as parents and setting/school leaders, as well as ensuring that the incentive does not put pressure on participants to sign up and/or continue on the project.

Harm Arising From Participation In, and Use of, Research

The main consideration for many research projects is the avoidance of harm to participants. In education research, it is difficult to imagine a project that would involve the necessary risk of harm to participants, whereas in medical research, it might be easier to envisage drug trials with risks of harm. However, harm can be done to participants in any research involving humans. For example, trialling a new maths intervention with one group of children, while withholding it from another group, could harm the second group in terms of their progress and learning, and where we are trialling an intervention or change that we have good reason to believe will be successful, a plan to offer 'catch up' for other groups is an ethical choice.

Using Research of Others in Our Practice

When using the research of others, it is very important to consider how the researchers have addressed ethical issues such as consent, harm and privacy. Sometimes it is difficult to ascertain this, but if the research is in an academic journal, often the institutional ethical approval has been confirmed before it is published. It is important to think about ethics when applying the research of others in your own practice. Some research projects are impossible to replicate in your own setting, for example, where laboratory conditions have been used, and sometimes research has been carried out in vastly different situations from yours. An example of this is when research has been carried out with undergraduate students to find out the best method for teaching them a specific new concept in Psychology. The research may have found that students respond best to an expert, lengthy explanation in a lecture style, followed by their own practical application of the concept in the lab, and revisiting the concept as part of an academic assignment. This may not work for teaching other concepts, or for teaching young children, and application of the findings of the research without adaptation and careful consideration of the differences in the research and your own setting could conceivably result in harm to the children's learning and a waste of time and effort for you. Chapter 4 gives further information on how to use ethically sourced research in your everyday work.

Below is a checklist (Fig. 5.1) that you may want to use to make sure you have considered the basics of research ethics for your

Researcher Checklist	
• If you are a student, working in a university, college, setting or school, have you checked the local ethical approval requirements?	
• Plan your research project design; without a research design you cannot assess the ethical requirements and risks (see chapter **).	
• Consider who your participants will be, and ethical implications for this group (e.g. are they vulnerable? Are there power issues between you and this group?)	
• Have you considered participant consent, withdrawal, privacy, data and harm?	
• Do you know who to signpost participants to for support?	
• Are you clear about when you would need to disclose participant information and data, for example if a participant admitted to a crime during an interview?	
• Have you created clear information sheets and consent forms for your participants?	
• Think about how you will handle the data, from collection to deletion.	
• Who will support you during the research project?	
• Consider your self-care and how you will ensure the research does no harm to you.	

Fig. 5.1. Researcher Ethics Checklist.

project. Any local ethical guidelines (such as those set by your university, college or employer) must be adhered to.

RESEARCHER SELF-CARE

I would always recommend that if you are conducting research, you consider your own care as seriously as you consider that of your participants, and that you really carefully consider your own self-care as a researcher. Research projects can be long, tiring, and participants can cover traumatic and triggering situations, even if the research project is on a seemingly innocuous topic. Think beforehand about what support services you can signpost for participants, and have these ready to share if you need to – but also think about the support you may need, and get that in place before you start. If you are carrying out research as a student or member of staff, make sure you know who to contact for help. Make sure your supervisor, personal tutor or line manager (if appropriate) understands that you may need some support, and if you are part of a group, make sure you support each other by being research buddies. If you are an independent researcher, there are independent researcher support groups; some of these are detailed in the Further Reading section at the end of the chapter.

Of course, you have to be careful about not sharing information about your participants that would breach your ethical approval, but if you can talk to someone about the impact of the research on you, you do not have to feel alone with what you have heard (Quickfall & Wood, 2025).

REFLECTIVE QUESTIONS

- Why are research ethics an important consideration for researchers? What are the potential dangers of not working ethically as a researcher?
- How can you ensure that your research project is being conducted ethically? If you are using the research of others to inform your practice, how can you check that this has been conducted ethically, and that your application of their findings is ethical?
- How can you protect yourself as a researcher? Why is this important?

REAL-LIFE ETHICS

In the following case study, you will find some of the themes we have been considering 'played out' in a real-life situation. Often in research, as in working in education more generally, the unexpected and unplanned will happen, as it did here.

As you read the case study, consider how this researcher:

- Responded to the dilemmas as they arose.
- Gained understanding of the context during the research data collection.
- Recognised the omissions from the original research design.
- Applied what they had found out to improve the ethical approaches used.

> **CASE STUDY: WORKING WITH KEY STAGE 1 AND FOUNDATION STAGE PARTICIPANTS**
>
> *As you read through this case study, consider how the researcher, John, has met (or not met)www the ethical requirements detailed in the first half of this chapter. Would you have done anything differently?*
>
> Some researchers are lucky enough to work on research projects where children are the participants, and in this case, the project aimed to find out if philosophy clubs (commonly used with older children and young people) could be effective with foundation stage and Key Stage 1 children in England (aged 4–7 years old). This phase of the project involved the researcher (I am going to call him John, but this isn't his real name) going into a school every week for 12 weeks to spend 1 hour facilitating a philosophical inquiry session with a group of 6–9 children. John was a student researcher at the time, and this was his first experience of research, but he was an experienced classroom teacher in upper Key Stage 2 and Key Stage 3 (children aged 9–14 years old). John had a keen interest in philosophy with children and had run clubs with older children as part of his teacher role, so he felt confident to undertake the practicalities of the project.
>
> In advance of the weekly sessions commencing, John had undergone all the necessary safeguarding checks required for working with children, had gained consent from the head

teacher, parents of the children and the class teachers involved, and had produced information sheets for these groups (Fig. 5.2). John also sent to the school some PowerPoint slides explaining philosophical inquiry in an age appropriate style for the children to watch to help them decide if they wanted to take part. John also had permission to collect photographs and audio recordings, and he also planned to take field notes during the sessions. A spare classroom was organised for the sessions.

Fig. 5.2. Example of Materials Designed for Child Participants.

Part of the research design was the safeguarding of the children who participated in the research, and as you would expect, John had followed a detailed process for any disclosures of abuse made by children during the philosophy sessions, and for the researcher to raise concerns about anything that did not seem right, or that were a worry. John was a student researcher, and the project was part of his Master's degree in Education, so he had a supervisor who was an experienced researcher at the university who had supported him with ethical approval and research design. However, John had not considered in advance some of the more nuanced ethical issues that could arise from this work, or how researching with young children may test some of the standard ethical guidelines that were designed, tried and tested on adults over the last century.

The Dilemmas

Consent and Ongoing Consent

John found that in each weekly session, some children would prefer not to take part on that occasion, perhaps because something exciting was happening in the classroom, but would expect to be invited to the next session. This meant that sometimes, children had missed part of a series of linked sessions, and John was frustrated that this meant part of the session had to be spent on a 'catch up', and his data were impacted by this recap activity. John had not anticipated this, and his ethics approval detailed how participants could withdraw from participation, but not how they could jump back onto the project.

To resolve this, John spoke to his supervisor at the university, who recommended that John adapt his project to allow children to pause their involvement, and to check at every session that children were happy to take part. They also recommended that John be mindful that children might want to withdraw completely from the project and to liaise with their class teacher to ensure he had the best information possible, where this might be the case, as the children might prefer to talk to their teacher about this.

Inner Worlds and Emotional Impacts

John was surprised at how skilled the young children in the philosophy club were, as creative thinkers and articulate members of a community. Children often shared examples from their own lives as part of philosophical discussions, and John had also not anticipated how much these would affect him as a researcher. In one session, when the group was discussing how people change as they grow up, one girl, Olivia, talked about her grandma dying and the last few months of her life, when she underwent rapid and dramatic changes to her health. The other children in the group were saddened by this, and John himself was deeply moved, having lost his own granddad just a few weeks before the project began, and John was not sure whether he should 'close down' Olivia's story, or let her continue and address any upset or concerns afterwards. In John's consent forms and information for parents, he had explained that children would be sharing their views and experiences and that these may be emotionally triggering, but that he would intervene if topics were unsuitable and that appropriate actions would be taken if information shared needed to be passed on.

John did let Olivia finish her story, and the discussion moved on from there to less emotionally charged topics. John felt upset about the session, and when it finished, he contacted his supervisor and also a close friend. His supervisor reassured him that he had done the right thing, and to flag up Olivia's story with the class teacher so that they could follow this up with the child, if appropriate. His supervisor also advised John to consider what actions he would have taken if the story had upset Olivia or other children in the group, so he could be ready for this in subsequent sessions, and to re-evaluate his expectations of young children, given his experience of the session. John also talked to his close friend, without disclosing any confidential information about the project, and worked through his own feelings about what happened.

Sharing Data

John eventually finished the series of sessions and came away with a huge amount of data from the discussions and activities the children had taken part in, as well as a new appreciation of the inner worlds of young children. John has ethical permission to use the data for his dissertation and to present (in anonymised form) to his master's cohort, and for his supervisor to access the data if necessary. A week after the project finished, the head teacher of the school where John had collected his data contacted him to ask if she could have access to the data, as she was interested in what the children had said and wondered if there was anything that she could incorporate into wider school improvement and planning. John felt uncomfortable about this, as the head teacher had kindly granted him access to the school to undertake his research, but he was not sure his ethical clearance covered this sharing of data.

John consulted his supervisor and the BERA Ethical Guidelines. They quickly assured themselves that John did not have ethical permission to share these data with the head teacher, and that she had been made aware of the uses of the data at the outset of the project. John's supervisor contacted the head teacher to advise that once John's dissertation was published in the university library, the head teacher would be able to access it and read the findings for herself.

Consider how John and his supervisor worked through these ethical dilemmas:

- **Responded:** John responded to ethical dilemmas by seeking support and advice, and his supervisor responded to John and helped him navigate these dilemmas. The nuanced dilemmas that occurred hadn't been addressed completely in the ethical approval John went through, but with expert help, these could be navigated.
- **Gained:** John gained a huge amount of insight into the inner worlds of young children, something that he had not anticipated before the project. John also gained a new understanding of ethics in action; the dilemmas faced in the sessions had a real emotional impact, which is hard to imagine when filling in ethics approval forms before the project begins.
- **Recognised:** Both John and his supervisor recognised the value of ongoing ethical discussions, after approval; if you are about to undertake some research, make sure you have ongoing support even after you have got the formal 'go ahead' to get started. Having an understanding friend or colleague who you can speak to is also very helpful, and

> John recognised his own self-care need to talk through what had happened.
> **Applied:** John applied the ethical guidelines for his discipline to his project, and went back to these when he had a dilemma on the ground. John and his supervisor applied their knowledge and care to each dilemma.

CONCLUSION

In this chapter, we have considered the basics of research ethics and how important ethical research practices are. Whilst we have focused on conducting research, it is also vital to consider the ethical basis of research we apply to our practice, and also the ethical implications of that application. Sometimes, ethically sound research is misapplied to other situations, with harmful consequences.

I hope this chapter has been useful as part of your research journey and wish you well with your own research endeavours. Key to your success is making sure that you, as a researcher, are cared for; this means considering yourself and your needs as part of the ethics process, and making sure those who support you (formally and informally) know what you need. To avoid sleepless nights over research dilemmas, reach out for support at any stage of your research, like John did in our case study.

REVIEW OF CHAPTER OBJECTIVES

In this chapter, you have:

- Explored an introduction to the basic aspects of research ethics and the importance of ethical practices when carrying out and applying research.
- Considered how research can be carried out ethically in the classroom and with children.
- Reflected on the importance of self-care for researchers.

FURTHER READING AND RESOURCES

- BERA Ethics Guidelines 5th Edition (2024). https://www.bera.ac.uk/publication/ethical-guidelines-for-educational-research-fifth-edition-2024-online

For anyone researching education, this is the 'go to' set of ethical guidelines for the UK and for many other countries around the world.

- BERA Ethics Case Studies. https://www.bera.ac.uk/publication-series/research-ethics-case-studies-2024

These case studies link to the BERA Ethics Guidelines with examples of ethics in practice. If you found the case study in this chapter useful, check these out!

- The UK Research Integrity Office (UKRIO) advice. https://ukrio.org/our-work/get-advice-from-ukrio/answers-to-common-enquiries/advice-for-independent-researchers-and-small-charities/

The UKRIO share some helpful advice on researching independently, if you have no organisation (e.g. university) to support your ethical approval and research.

- The Social Research Association Ethics guidance and website. https://the-sra.org.uk/SRA/SRA/Ethics/Research-Ethics-Guidance.aspx?hkey=5e809828-fb49-42be-a17e-c95d6cc72da1

The Social Research Association website has lots of helpful advice, as well as its own ethics guidance. The SRA can also provide feedback on research ethics proposals (but there is a fee for this expert work).

REFERENCES

British Educational Research Association. (2024). *BERA ethics guidelines 5th edition*. https://www.bera.ac.uk/publication/ethical-guidelines-for-educational-research-fifth-edition-2024-online

British Psychological Society. (2021). Code of ethics and conduct. https://doi.org/10.53841/bpsrep.2021.inf94

British Sociological Association. (2017). Guidelines for *ethical research*. https://www.britsoc.co.uk/media/24310/bsa_statement_of_ethical_practice.pdf

Busher, H., & Fox, A. (2021). The amoral academy? A critical discussion of research ethics in the neo-liberal university. *Educational Philosophy and Theory*, *53*(5), 469–478. https://doi.org/10.1080/00131857.2019.1707656

Head, G. (2020). Ethics in educational research: Review boards, ethical issues and researcher development. *European Educational Research Journal*, *19*(1), 72–83. https://doi-org.oclc.org/10.1177/1474904118796315

Mauthner, M., Birch, M., Miller, T., & Jessop, J. (2012). Conclusion: Navigating ethical dilemmas and new digital horizons. In T. Miller, M. Birch, M. Mauthner, & J. Jessop (Eds.), *Ethics in qualitative research* (2nd ed., pp. 176–186). SAGE Publications Ltd. https://doi.org/10.4135/9781473913912

Miller, T., & Bell, L. (2012). Consenting to what? Issues of access, gatekeeping and 'informed' consent. In T. Miller, M. Birch, M. Mauthner, & J. Jessop (Eds.), *Ethics in qualitative research* (2nd ed., pp. 61–75). SAGE Publications Ltd. https://doi.org/10.4135/9781473913912

Quickfall, A. (2022). Reflecting on ethical processes and dilemmas in doctoral research. *Education Sciences*, *12*(11), 751. https://doi.org/10.3390/educsci12110751

Quickfall, A., & Wood, P. (2025). *Interviewing online: Ethic of care and protecting participants and researchers using unstructured interviews*. SAGE Research Methods. https://doi.org/10.4135/9781036213282

Social Research Association. (2021). *Research ethics guidance*. https://the-sra.org.uk/SRA/SRA/Ethics/Research-Ethics-Guidance.aspx?hkey=5e809828-fb49-42be-a17e-c95d6cc72da1

6

SUSTAINABILITY: RESEARCH AND REALITY IN THE EDUCATION DEBATE

Leigh Hoath[a] and Heena Dave[b]

[a]Leeds Trinity University, UK
[b]Climate Adapted Pathways for Education, UK

CHAPTER OBJECTIVES

In this chapter, you will:

- Examine the evolution of education for sustainable development (ESD) in England.
- Critically evaluate the challenges of integrating sustainability and climate change education (CCE) in schools.
- Explore the balance between conceptual knowledge, participatory engagement, and action-oriented learning in effective ESD practices.
- Reflect on strategies to support hope and emotional resilience in the face of climate anxiety amongst learners.
- Identify evidence-informed approaches to curriculum design that empower teachers and pupils to take meaningful action.

Keywords: Research informed practice; climate change education (CCE); sustainability; education for sustainable development (ESD); climate anxiety

INTRODUCTION

This chapter picks up a topic which is positioned within education as being of paramount importance for the future of the planet, but one which is met with inconsistency in the school system and the wider education sector (Jowett, 2024).

There is a history of attempts to move sustainability and CCE higher on the priority list for policymakers and teachers, which will be touched upon later within this chapter. There is an increasing range of resources available, but these are insufficient on their own. This chapter will position the need for high-quality implementation and curriculum making with respect to these areas (Hoath & Dave, 2024).

The chapter will also draw attention to some of the common pitfalls with respect to teaching about sustainability and climate change and offer suggestions on how these can be avoided to support our children and young people in dealing with and addressing the climate crisis.

THE NEED FOR SUSTAINABILITY AND CCE

Average temperature changes have increased over the last decades, with the highest average temperature being recorded in 2024 globally (Hawkins et al., 2025; Met Office, 2025). Hawkins, a climate scientist from the University of Reading, created the 'Climate Stripes' visualisation, which depicts the average temperature changes since the late 1800s. This serves as a powerful and accessible presentation of climate change over time, and brings an abstract concept to life in the classroom.

Although there are some climate change deniers within all communities, there is overwhelming evidence that anthropogenically induced climate change is the greatest factor in the temperature increases illustrated by Hawkins' stripes (IPCC, 2022).

The environmental and societal impacts are becoming increasingly obvious. For instance, in 2024, Venezuela was the first country in the Americas to lose all its glaciers (Camacho, 2024). Similarly, more frequent storms and inclement weather over our last two winters here in the UK and flooding here and globally have also impacted people's lives, and increased awareness more broadly (Kendon et al., 2024).

Eco-Anxieties

The Children's Society (n.d.) undertakes an annual survey, 'The Good Childhood Report', of 10- to 17-year-olds in the UK, which asks children about the worries in their lives. In 2022, the environment was at the top of the worry list, with 75% of respondents being a little to very worried about it. In 2023, the survey reported 72% feeling the same (second in the list of concerns) and 69% in 2024 (third in the list). Worries about rising prices and crime have taken the top spot, but the environment remains in the top four anxieties throughout those years. These anxieties are also felt by children across other countries. In 2021, Hickman et al. surveyed 10,000 16- to 25-year-olds across 10 countries, including the UK, and found that 84% of respondents were moderately or extremely worried about climate change. Whilst, as Léger-Goodes et al. (2022) argue, these anxieties about climate, crime and inequalities are an entirely natural response, they do highlight that pupils are facing multiple crises – often referred to as a polycrisis. Their everyday lives, at school and at home, are shaped by the ways we all respond to, manage and mitigate the impacts of this crisis.

Gaps in the Curriculum

British Science Association and the University of Plymouth (2023) reported that 70% of 14- to 18-year-olds wanted the opportunity to learn more about climate change. The British Science Association (BSA) also argued that this focus should run across subjects, and not be simply left to science and geography, as is often the case. Evidence suggests that pupils' concerns about climate change and sustainability, and the BSA's recognition of the importance of those concerns being addressed across the curriculum, are not yet being sufficiently recognised in practice. Greer et al.'s (2024) survey of pupils' experiences of the curriculum found that:

- 37% say that climate change is 'sometimes' mentioned in their school, and 35.9% 'sometimes' mention sustainability.
- Sustainability and climate change are most often included in science and geography.

This culminates in a strong argument and responsibility that there is a need to educate our children and young people about climate change, in a way that engenders hope, collective action and change in behaviours which will support the adaptation and mitigation required to protect the planet.

EDUCATION FOR SUSTAINABLE DEVELOPMENT

The ways in which climate change is impacting pupils' lives, and the increase in associated anxieties, mean that sustainability and climate change have evoked responses from international organisations such as the United Nations and United Nations Educational, Scientific and Cultural Organisation (UNESCO). This response has mainly been in the form of curriculum policies and guidelines that have become known as ESD (UNESCO, 2020, 2021; United Nations, 2021). This approach has culminated in the *Greening Curriculum Guidance* (UNESCO, 2024).

For the purpose of this chapter, we will consider the very latest and internationally formalised UNESCO definition, where they state that ESD should teach:

- Individuals to make informed decisions and take action, both individually and collectively, to change society and protect the planet.
- Equips people of all ages with the knowledge, skills, values, and ability to tackle issues such as climate change, biodiversity loss, overuse of resources, and inequality that impact the well-being of people and the planet.

UNESCO positions ESD as the way to approach sustainability and CCE, but retaining a focus on the environment, society and economy. For instance, the UNESCO (2022) Greening Education Partnerships website aims to ensure that every learner is climate-ready. The focus on ESD, which emphasises individuals' choices and lifestyles, ignores the need for a climate change and sustainability curriculum which addresses issues of values, collective action and the costs of development as well as its benefits. In addition, ESD neglects to consider subject specificity and disciplinary knowledge.

ESD, Policy, and Schools in England

The notion of teaching and learning about sustainability and CCE through ESD is not new. ESD in the UK has gone through many iterations, although it continues to be misaligned with the currently prominent knowledge-rich curricula ideology. This makes implementation challenging. There has been significant change and periods of important investment and retrenchment in these areas over the last 25 years, and yet this remains a real issue in terms of the priority of sustainability and CCE being implemented. As such, our understanding of this needs to be within the social, economic, but particularly the curricular policy contexts of each period (Greer & Glackin, 2021; Shedrake et al., 2025), which are summarised in Table 6.1.

In 2004, then Prime Minister Tony Blair stated that

> *Sustainability and climate change will not just be a subject in the classroom: It will be in its bricks and mortar and the way the school uses and even generates its own power. Our pupils won't just be told about climate change, they will see and work within it. A living, learning, place in which to explore what a sustainable lifestyle means.*
> *(Blair, 2004)*

This statement outlines some of the key themes, and key promises that have formed shifting policy in England. It explicitly positions sustainability as part of a 'lifestyle', a continuing focus on individuals' consuming, working and learning, perhaps at the expense of community action and activism (Greer & Glackin, 2021). It also

Table 6.1. Timeline of ESD Policy and Practice in English Education.

1960s and 1970s	Growing awareness of the environmental impact of economic activity and the beginnings of intergovernmental discussions. Individual teachers with personal interests take advantage of curricular autonomy to focus on the environment
1980s	New policies are designed to increase accountability and teaching standards, and to standardise curricular entitlements, such as the 1988 National Curriculum. Environmental concerns become marginalised as they are subsumed into subjects, and as attention shifts to outcomes
1990s	Increasing international focus on climate change and the environment leads to governmental 'rebranding' of environmental education to ESD, framed by ideas of human growth and economic development and focussed on the improvement of quality of life
1998	The New Labour government set up the Sustainable Development Education Panel, which was designed with principles for ESD curriculum development, which included a broader focus on community, diversity, and environmental stewardship
2004	The Environmental Audit Committee released a report, 'The Sustainable Development Strategy: Illusion or Reality?', which criticised the government's inconsistent approach to sustainability, especially when this conflicted with economic development, and in the piecemeal approach to ESD
2005	The UK Government Sustainable Development Strategy was published, which clarified and concentrated the policy approach into five key principles. A budget of £12m allocated to the climate change communications initiative
2006	Sustainable schools initiative launched, including non-compulsory guidance about integrating ESD across the curriculum
2009	The ESD report, released by Ofsted, which critiques the impact of ESD in schools as limited and uneven. Teachers continue to be largely burdened with the implementation of ESD without training or support

2010–2014	The coalition government closes the sustainable schools initiative, within a larger reform of the curriculum. The new policy strips out most ESD and sustainability content, and although ESD remains in Science and (after debate) in Geography, it is removed from Citizenship and cross-curricular themes
2015–2020	Increasing international activity (including the promotion of ESD policies outlined above) and the declaration of a climate emergency in parliament are not matched by curricular reform in England. ESD remains a low priority, though individual teachers, schools, and other forms of activism reflect growing public debate (and division)
2020–2024	Schools and teachers continue to develop ESD initiatives and curricular responses, but the national curriculum is unreformed, and ESD remains the isolated focus of sub-elements within each subject
2025	The curriculum and assessment review was announced by the incoming Labour Government. Many responses to the call for evidence envisage a threading of ESD issues through the curriculum

envisages an ESD approach within a cross curricular framework, which carries with it some advantages and disadvantages, but depends on support for implementation in training, accountability, resourcing and space for curricular innovation. As we can also see from the table above despite ESD reaching a policy peak under Blair's government, implementation was largely uneven and often superficial. Through no fault of their own teachers have consistently lacked training, support, or incentives, and as a result whilst some schools became models, most lagged behind in addressing the teaching of these important, existential issues.

Is There a Poor Fit Between ESD and Education?

Despite the scope of Blair's statement, and the 20-plus years since his speech, which included UNESCO announcing the 'Decade of Education for Sustainable Development' (DESD) from 2005 to

2014, policy and practice have been ineffective at meeting this ambition. Some practitioners argue that overall ESD in England 'has singularly failed to improve the sustainability consciousness (SC) of young people' and that over their time in school pupils become less interested in sustainability (Macpherson, 2019). A recent survey by the Department for Education (DfE) and Royal Meterological Society (Fleetwood et al., 2024) suggests that there are significant gaps in the climate literacy of young people, including fundamental knowledge such as the impact of the 1.5°C/2°C warming. The report also suggests that other key climate change concepts, including Net Zero, a 'phrase in widespread use, from politicians to schools, employers and the media', are subject to a 'surprising and concerning' confusion.

The concept of 'sustainability' itself also presents problems, because it means very different things in different contexts (Vogt & Weber, 2019). For instance, in a business setting, financial or organisational sustainability might be at the fore of people's thinking. Whilst there are often common threads in understanding environmental concepts of sustainability across cultures, there are also differences (Throsby & Petetskaya, 2016), and some indigenous cultures do not acknowledge this as a word at all. The need to reflect these varied conceptualisations of a word that is commonly used adds to the complexity of planning and teaching around ESD goals.

International evidence suggests that the lack of impact of ESD is also an issue in other countries. Sass et al. (2023), who studied the ability, motivation, and confidence of young people in Belgium and Flanders to take meaningful action towards sustainability found that teaching of sustainability that included a focus on the 'how' of sustainability – action, and on real-world relevance, was more effective than 'holistic' teaching which focussed more on the 'what' through inter-disciplinary concepts. They also found that, generally, pupils' levels of confidence in their sustainability agency were not being impacted by school.

Time constraints in England's schools limit teachers' capacity for professional dialogue and research. This is especially crucial for sustainability and CCE, given the urgency of the climate crisis (Hoath & Dave, 2022). Furthermore, these times and curriculum constraints can often lead to ESD becoming sidelined in extracurricular or optional activities. This common 'cafeteria of experience' (Wal, 2018) approach disadvantages children from lower-income backgrounds, as this equity gap arises as more privileged students find it easier to take advantage of these opportunities (Wal, 2018).

The United Nations Sustainable Development Goals (UNSDGs) (United Nations, 2015) are often used as a framework in schools to support the teaching and learning of sustainability and climate change. It is not unusual to see a display which shows the 17 goals as a table. These goals outline a framework that attempts to significantly improve responses to climate change and environmental damage, poverty, and conflict. This framework sits within broader UN aims focussed on educational disadvantage, inclusion and more equitable economic development. Despite the focus on the UNSDGs in many schools around the world, the efforts of dedicated teachers to integrate these into their teaching, and the impetus of many governments, the United Nations (2024) found that progress falls far short of what is required to meet the UNSDGs and only 17% of the goals are displaying sufficient improvements if they are to meet the target date of 2030.

Some have argued that the UNSDGs design as a global development initiative means they are not suitable for being used as a framework for reform of curriculum and pedagogy. Simply transplanting the SDG framework into schools risks oversimplifying education and overlooking the fundamental purposes of education (Eilam, 2025). Similarly, ESD curriculum policy has tended to ignore tensions between economic growth and sustainability (Glavic, 2020; Kopnina, 2020). These challenges can mean that ESD's curricular aims become un-clear, and that they also continue to place responsibility for sustainability and climate change at the level of individual pupils, in the way that they make 'choices' about their careers, their consumption and their 'lifestyles' (Greer & Glackin, 2021), which has obvious implications for their well-being and anxiety.

Without providing clear educational goals that relate specifically to sustainability and climate change, rather than generic ESD, approaches will remain fragmented. The knowledge-rich emphasis in the current National Curriculum (NC) in England on disciplinary conceptual knowledge risks a conflict between the intent of the official curriculum with the tradition and aims of ESD. As we have seen, evidence suggests that there needs to be a balance between the conceptual propositional resources favoured by the knowledge-rich approach and the participatory and action-focussed emphasis implied by the ESD tradition (Sass et al., 2023).

Further challenges arise from the nature of teaching itself. Alvunger (2021) suggests that classrooms are complex due to the variation in individuals within them, what everyone brings to schools with them in terms of attitudes and beliefs and then a layer of everyday life on top of those. Biesta (2009) develops this perspective with the argument that educational goals are themselves complex, overlapping and sometimes in tension – especially when pupils' individual interests, concerns, and experiences are taken into account.

These challenges also extend to teacher confidence and subject knowledge. All primary school teachers in England will have a General Certificate of Secondary Education (GCSE) science qualification (or equivalent), only 43% of primary school science leads have a science A-level, and many primary teachers lack confidence in their science content knowledge (Wellcome Trust, 2017). Greer et al. (2024, p. 20) discovered teachers themselves most frequently use 'films and videos', 'news media', 'resources that I create', and 'online resources provided by external organisations' to support teaching related to sustainability and/or climate change – suggesting the risk that these resources might reflect broader confusions or misconceptions of wider society. An important proportion of this knowledge is science-related, which presents a challenge for many secondary and primary teachers (Greer et al., 2024). This lack of accurate knowledge about ESD is reflected in research, which has found that a third of responding teachers reported that they were not very or at all confident in teaching about climate change (Gillow et al., 2022).

Overall, this means that we need to be wary of the way that 'sustainability' – and 'being sustainable' – are presented as a solution to individuals' problems and global crises. Especially when we are asked to base curricula on 'development goals' outside of the realm of education, we need to recognise the complexity of the issues and to carefully avoid oversimplifying our response. One clear implication of the challenges is the need for curricula to have a developmental balance between foundational knowledge – for both teachers and pupils – and the enabling and motivating effects of participation and action. These need to be progressively secured and built on for a deepening understanding about, and confidence and orientation towards the environment.

> **REFLECTIVE QUESTIONS**
>
> - What are the limitations of the approaches to ESD that curriculum policy has so far taken?
>
> - What kinds of knowledge and skills can a specific subject, or your teaching, bring to teaching specifically about climate change? Think about:
>   - Disciplinary Knowledge – the specific links with subjects and climate change.
>   - Metacognition and self-regulation – how can teaching take place to ensure that learners have the time to reflect and articulate their thinking and feelings?
>   - Collection action – of influence, advocacy, making and doing?
>
> - What will be your next steps in reviewing evidence or research in relation to sustainability and climate change?

Overcoming the Challenges – Hope and Guidance

Having considered the challenges to the implementation of sustainability and CCE into school curricula, we want to make some suggestions about ways to address them. This is not a one-size-fits-all solution. Instead, we suggest some principles which can be used to develop responses to your individual contexts.

We want to start by returning to the issue of eco-anxiety that we highlighted in the introduction, because we would like to suggest a role for 'hope'. Hickman et al. (2021) report that eco-anxiety is increasingly common amongst children and teenagers, and we started by recognising the responsibility that this places on us as educators. In response to these anxieties, Ojala (2017) argues that we can promote a hopeful outlook. Importantly, her argument reflects the research we have discussed above, and the importance of a balance between conceptual, participatory, and action-focussed curriculum planning.

Ojala (2017) writes that it is vital to promote a hopeful outlook concerning this problem and humanity's ability to mitigate it, but her argument is not simply that we should make pupils feel better or dismiss their concerns. She puts forward a role for 'constructive hope', which is action-orientated and builds on existing strengths, as well as focusing on achievable goals. Therefore, it is important that the curriculum reflects a balance to be struck by you as a teacher – being able to plan for mitigating eco-anxiety through self-regulation and enabling a hopeful outlook, but without giving overly optimistic false hope, which Marlon et al. (2019) state leads to disillusionment and inaction. Similarly, Malboeuf-Hurtubise et al. (2024) propose the development of 'radical hope', which embraces the uncertainty of outcome at the same time as commitment to action. They suggest several steps which offer routes into curriculum and activity planning, with the aim of working through and with hope:

- Recognising and accepting these emotions, especially in children.
- Providing skills and resources to support and promote coping strategies.
- Guiding children towards constructive actions. Using activities and resources that promote emotional well-being to prevent activist burnout.

This focus on radical, but carefully planned and scaffolded hope, implies a range of actions, support and resources that teachers will need.

Teacher Knowledge
First amongst these is accurate and up-to-date climate change and environmental knowledge, which will enable careful use of

language, selection of curricular goals, activities and resources associated with sustainability and climate change. Teachers will also need this knowledge to justify the alignment of sustainability and climate change issues within existing curricula in school settings. This enhanced knowledge should also support teachers in developing sustainability and CCE, which is integrated into the core learning experiences in school, so as to avoid the inequity of the extra-curricular 'cafeteria' approach, and benefit all students.

Supported, Collective Flexibility
Together, this implies a need for curriculum flexibility. Flexibility is required by the planning of careful, radical hope, and the development of resources and content which are carefully contextualised for your own setting.

However, we also know that curriculum flexibility can have an impact on teachers' already limited time and their well-being (Hulme et al., 2024, 2025). To support teachers in gaining this knowledge and making decisions, a number of organisations and resources are springing up. For instance, there are Climate Adapted Pathways for Education (CAPE) Alliance, which the authors have set up to provide guidance and Continuing Professional Development (CPD) for teachers and schools, is one such organisation, and there are others.

However, teachers will also need time and collaborative spaces to:

- Explore the reasons for including specific elements (Biesta, 2009) and how this relates to their subject or classroom, as well as the context of their pupils and school settings.
- Grasp key concepts and misconceptions about sustainability, climate change, and environment.
- Consider the (sometimes contested) meanings of specific terms.
- Use criteria to evaluate the quality, benefits and costs of resources they are asked to use.
- Evaluate the impact of their planning and teaching on curricular aims, but also on the anxieties and capacities for action that the research suggests are so important in climate change education.

We hope that these resources and spaces might be provided in schools, across multi-academy trusts (MAT), federations or alliances of schools, through subject associations and subject community resources (see Hawkey, 2023), for an example, from the History subject community), or from further professional development or education. We recognise, however, that there is a lack of resources and funds to support their creation and use.

REFLECTIVE QUESTIONS

- Why do you think it is important to engage with current research around sustainability and CCE?

- How can you engage with the research around pedagogy and practice of teaching these areas?

- After reading this chapter, what do you consider the most important factors for your setting to research and use for an evidence-informed approach?

CASE STUDY

Miriam is an Early Career Teacher (ECT) primary teacher at Greenfields School, and after some CPD given by the Geography curriculum team at the BrightStar Multi Academy Trust, has decided she wants to do more on the climate crisis with her Year 3 class. The CPD introduced UNSDGs, and also the 'Climate Stripes' (Hawkins et al., 2025), which she thought were a really interesting way of highlighting the issues.

Miriam has noticed that her pupils have been discussing their worries about climate change in lots of different topics. She has been worried that this was getting in the way of their curriculum objectives. So, she was hoping to dedicate sessions at the end of four Friday afternoons to creating posters about climate change, as a way of addressing those worries, but also so these issues might not take up so much time on other days.

Miriam introduced the activity by showing a brief video explaining all 17 UNSDGs and invited the group to work in small groups to pick one of the goals and create an informational poster using the internet for research. Some pupils chose to illustrate their posters vividly, but others copied text directly from websites they found difficult to understand. Sarah noticed a group of pupils chose goals unrelated to climate change or sustainability, such as 'Poverty', but they seemed to get a lot out of the activity and looked forward to Friday afternoons when they got to work on their posters.

Because she did not have time to carefully check the posters, she decided that the last afternoon would be an 'exhibition', followed by a class debate about which of these goals is most important. Their decision would be followed up by a letter to their head teacher, with a request that the school curriculum be developed so that it focusses on this key goal more than it does at present.

At the end of the month, the debate went well, letters were written, and afterwards, posters were displayed in the corridor. Whilst her pupils felt proud, Miriam started to feel unsure if the project had deepened their understanding of climate change or addressed their anxieties.

REFLECTIVE QUESTIONS

- How would you evaluate Miriam's curricular aims for this project?
- Do you think Miriam's plans reflected the need for a balance between disciplinary knowledge, metacognition and self-regulation, and collective action?
- Do you think these plans properly addressed the seriousness of the issues?
- What do you think was the impact on the eco-anxieties of Miriam's pupils?

CONCLUSION

We hope that this chapter has underlined an ongoing responsibility for teachers and researchers to consider the needs of our pupils in response to the climate crisis. We also hope that we have alerted you to some of the challenges associated with sustainability and climate change education, but also considered how they can be addressed in the context of your school settings.

Finally, we want to give you grounds and ideas for hope. Our hope is that in helping you prepare for the barriers, and alerting you to the need for educational experiences which use a curriculum balanced between knowledge, participation and action, you feel more able, and justified to plan curricula that teach powerful knowledge, and which create powerful learning opportunities for discussion, discovery, self-regulation, and collective action.

REVIEW OF CHAPTER OBJECTIVES

In this chapter, you have:

- Examined the evolution of ESD in England.

- Critically evaluated the challenges of integrating sustainability and CCE in schools.

- Explored the balance between conceptual knowledge, participatory engagement, and action-oriented learning in effective ESD practices.

- Reflected on strategies to support hope and emotional resilience in the face of climate anxiety amongst learners.

- Identified evidence-informed approaches to curriculum design that empower teachers and pupils to take meaningful action.

FURTHER READING AND RESOURCES

Hoath, L., & Dave, H. (2022). *Sustainability and climate change education: Creating the foundations for effective implementation*. Leeds Trinity University and the Teacher Development Trust.

Hoath, L., & Dave, H. (2024). *Implementing climate change education in schools: Constructive hope in action*. Climate Adapted Pathways for Education and Leeds Trinity University.

REFERENCES

Alvunger, D. (2021). Curriculum making and knowledge conceptions in classrooms in the context of standards-based curricula. *The Curriculum Journal, 32*, 607–625. https://doi.org/10.1002/curj.108

Biesta, G. (2009). Good education in an age of measurement: On the need to reconnect with the question of purpose in education. *Educational Assessment, Evaluation and Accountability (Formerly: Journal of Personnel Evaluation in Education), 21*(1), 33–46.

Blair, T. (2004, September 15). *Blair's climate change speech*. https://www.theguardian.com/politics/2004/sep/15/greenpolitics.uk

British Science Association and the University of Plymouth. (2023). *Climate change in secondary schools: Young people's views of climate change education*. Future Forum. Retrieved August 1, 2025, from https://www.britishscienceassociation.org/Handlers/Download.ashx?IDMF=68f84964-bf1e-4bfb-8205-444705d9678a

Camacho, F. (2024, July 19). At least two countries have lost all their glaciers. *Scientific American*. Retrieved April 24, 2025, from https://www.scientificamerican.com/article/at-least-two-countries-have-lost-all-their-glaciers/

Eilam, E. (2025). Interrogating climate change education epistemology: Identifying hindrances to curriculum development. *ECNU Review of Education, 8*(1), 112–143. https://doi.org/10.1177/20965311241240491

Fleetwood, S., Hayes, L., Ozan, J., Knight, S., & Department for Education. (2024). *Climate literacy amongst school leavers*. By Royal

Meteorological Society & Ipsos. Retrieved April 24, 2025, from https://assets.publishing.service.gov.uk/media/67616fecf666d2e4faef3972/Climate_Literacy_School_Leavers_2024.pdf

Gillow, E., Schwitzer, R., & Dorrell, E. (2022). *Teaching about climate change: A report in climate change and sustainability education in schools*. Public First.

Glavic, P. (2020). Identifying key issues of education for sustainable development. *Sustainability*, *12*, 6500–6518. https://doi.org/10.3390/su12166500

Greer, K., & Glackin, M. (2021). 'What counts' as climate change education? Perspectives from policy influencers. *School Science Review*, *103*(383), 15–22.

Greer, K., Walshe, N., Kitson, A., & Dillon, J. (2024). Responding to the environmental emergency through education: The imperative for teacher support across all subjects. *UCL Open Environment*, *6*(1). https://doi.org/10.14324/111.444/ucloe.1987

Hawkey, K. (2023). *History and the climate crisis: Environmental history in the classroom*. UCL Press. https://doi.org/10.2307/jj.4329862

Hoath, L., & Dave, H. (2022). *Sustainability and climate change education: Creating the foundations for effective implementation*. Leeds Trinity University and The Teacher Development Trust.

Hawkins, E., Williams, R.G., Young, P., Berardelli, J., Burgess, S., Highwood, E., Randel, W., Roussenov, V., Smoth, D., & Woods Placky, B. (2025). Warming stripes spark climate conversations: from the ocean to the stratosphere. *Bulletin of the American Meteorological Society, 106(5)*, E964–E970. https://doi.org/10.1175/BAMS-D-24-0212.1

Hickman, C., Marks, E., Pihkala, P., Clayton, S., Lewandowski, R.E., Mayall, E.., Wray, B., Mellor, C., & van Susteran, L. (2021). Climate anxiety in children and young people and their beliefs about government responses to climate change: a global survey. *The Lancet Planetary Health*, *5*(12), 863–873.

Hoath, L., & Dave, H. (2024). *Implementing climate change education in schools: Constructive hope in action*. Climate Adapted Pathways for Education and Leeds Trinity University.

Hulme, M., Beauchamp, G., Wood, J., & Bignell, C. (2024). *Teacher workload research report 2024*. Retrieved April 24, 2025, from https://www.researchgate.net/profile/Moira-Hulme-2/publication/381301623_Teacher_Workload_Research_Report_2024_Main_Report/links/6666f4ca85a4ee7261b399fd/Teacher-Workload-Research-Report-2024-Main-Report.pdf

Hulme, M., Beauchamp, G., Wood, J., & Bignell, C. (2025). Workload intensification and wellbeing among primary school teachers in Scotland. *Education 3-13*, 1–14. https://doi.org/10.1080/03004279.2024.2448509

IPCC. (2022). Climate change 2022: Impacts, adaptation and vulnerability. In H.-O. Pörtner, D. C. Roberts, M. Tignor, E. S. Poloczanska, K. Mintenbeck, A. Alegría, M. Craig, S. Langsdorf, S. Löschke, V. Möller, A. Okem, & B. Rama (Eds.), *Contribution of Working Group II to the sixth assessment report of the intergovernmental panel on climate change* (p. 3056). Cambridge University Press. https://doi.org/10.1017/9781009325844

Jowett, L. (2024). *I've spent a year speaking to schools—Here's why climate change must be in the new national curriculum* [Blog]. Climate Action in South Yorkshire Schools and Education Settings. https://research.shu.ac.uk/sustainability/2024/11/22/ive-spent-a-year-speaking-to-schools-heres-why-climate-change-must-be-in-the-new-national-curriculum/

Kendon, M., Doherty, A., Hollis, D., Carlisle, E., Packman, S., McCarthy, M., Jevrejeva, S., Matthews, A., Williams, J., Garforth, J., & Sparks, T. (2024). State of the UK Climate 2023. *International Journal of Climatology*, 44(S1), 1–117. https://doi.org/10.1002/joc.8553

Kopnina, H. (2020). Education for the future? Critical evaluation of education for sustainable development goals. *The Journal of Environmental Education*, 51(4), 280–291. https://doi.org/10.1080/00958964.2019.1710444

Léger-Goodes, T., Malboeuf-Hurtubise, C., Mastine, T., Généreux, M., Paradis, P.-O., & Camden, C. (2022). Eco-anxiety in children: A scoping review of the mental health impacts of the awareness of climate change. *Frontiers in Psychology*, 13, 872544. https://doi.org/10.3389/fpsyg.2022.872544

Macpherson, J. (2019). *Unsustain ED? Why ESD isn't working*. @Robin_Macp. https://robin-macpherson.com/2019/11/09/unsustained-why-esd-isnt-working/

Malboeuf-Hurtubise, C., Léger-Goodes, T., Herba, C. M., Bélanger, N., Smith, J., & Marks, E. (2024). Meaning making and fostering radical hope: Applying positive psychology to eco-anxiety research in youth. *Frontiers in Child and Adolescent Psychiatry, 3*. https://doi.org/10.3389/frcha.2024.1296446

Marlon, J. R., Bloodhart, B., Ballew, M. T., Rolfe-Redding, J., Roser-Renouf, C., Leiserowitz, A., & Maibach, E. (2019). How hope and doubt affect climate change mobilization. *Frontiers in Communication, 4*. https://doi.org/10.3389/fcomm.2019.00020

Met Office. (2025). *2024: Record-breaking watershed year for global climate*. Retrieved April 24, 2025, from https://www.metoffice.gov.uk/about-us/news-and-media/media-centre/weather-and-climate-news/2025/2024-record-breaking-watershed-year-for-global-climate

Ojala, M. (2017). Facing anxiety in climate change education: From therapeutic practice to hopeful transgressive learning. *Canadian Journal of Environmental Education, 21*, 41–56.

Sass, W., De Maeyer, S., Boeve-de Pauw, J., & Van Petegem, P. (2023). Effectiveness of education for sustainability: The importance of an action-oriented approach. *Environmental Education Research, 30*(4), 479–498. https://doi.org/10.1080/13504622.2023.2229543

Sheldrake, R., Walshe, N., & Hargreaves, E. (2025). Agentic action as an aim for sustainability education: Views from secondary school teachers in England. *Environmental Education Research, 31*(6), 1–18. https://doi.org/10.1080/13504622.2025.2464240

The Children's Society. (n.d.). *The good childhood report*. Retrieved April 24, 2025, from https://www.childrenssociety.org.uk/good-childhood

Throsby, D., & Petetskaya, E. (2016). Sustainability concepts in indigenous and non-indigenous cultures. *International Journal of Cultural Property, 23*(2), 119–140. https://doi.org/10.1017/S0940739116000084

UNESCO. (2020). *Education for sustainable development: A roadmap*. UNESCO. https://doi.org/10.54675/yfre1448

UNESCO. (2021). *Learn for our planet: A global review of how environmental issues are integrated in education; summary (ED/PSD/ESD/2021/02)*. UNESCO.

UNESCO. (2022). Greening education partnership. UNESCO. https://www.unesco.org/en/sustainable-development/education/greening-future

UNESCO. (2024). *Greening curriculum guidance – Teaching and learning for climate action*. UNESCO. https://doi.org/10.54675/aooz1758

UNITED NATIONS. (2015). *The 17 goals*. United Nations.

UNITED NATIONS. (2021). *Sustainable goals development report*. United Nations.

United Nations. (2024). *The sustainable development goals report 2024*. https://unstats.un.org/sdgs/report/2024/

Vogt, M., & Weber, C. (2019). Current challenges to the concept of sustainability. *Global Sustainability*, 2, e4. https://doi.org/10.1017/sus.2019.1

Wal, J. (2018). How the "cafeteria of experience" impacts our development. *Psychology Today* [online]. https://www.psychologytoday.com/za/blog/finding-the-next-einstein/201802/how-the-cafeteria-experience-impacts-our-development

Welcome Trust. (2017). *'State of the nation' report of UK primary science education. Welcome Trust and CFE research*. [online] Wellcome. https://wellcome.org/reports/state-nation-report-uk-primary-science-education.

7

PUPILS AS RESEARCHERS: EMPOWERING INQUIRY IN EDUCATION

Alison Griffiths and Jo Hopton

Leeds Trinity University, UK

CHAPTER OBJECTIVES

In this chapter, you will

- Consider what is meant by conducting research with pupils and explore its significance in fostering their confidence and agency.
- Examine the ethical implications that must be addressed before initiating any research project.
- Reflect on what constitutes an appropriate research question and discover methods that pupils can use to investigate and reach conclusions.
- Investigate how teachers can sensitively scaffold and facilitate exploration.

Keyword: Agency; access; advocacy; authenticity; collaboration; curiosity; ethics; philosophy for children

INTRODUCTION

When we think about research involving pupils, it's easy to imagine them as passive subjects who provide the data to support adult-designed research agendas. But what if we turned that notion on its head? Imagine a situation where pupils are not just participants but instead are active researchers, shaping the inquiry process with their unique perspectives and understandings of the world. In this chapter, we will explore how you can reimagine research with pupils as a dynamic, collaborative partnership, one that empowers them to take the lead, ask the questions that matter and engage them as true creators of knowledge.

We will explore how you can support pupils to engage in research and why this is such an important endeavour. We will consider how to create a climate of curiosity and inquiry in your classroom, examining the profound impact this can have on engagement. We will also explore the importance of crafting the right research question, providing examples of methods that pupils can use to investigate and find answers. The role of the teacher in fostering inquiry will be examined, offering practical advice on how to scaffold and guide this process effectively.

DEFINITIONS OF RESEARCH

Research is all around us, we encounter it daily in newspapers, on TV and on social media. News reports might claim, 'Research shows that eating vegetables makes us healthier' or 'Studies found that pupils who read every day perform better in tests'. On TV, we see programmes about scientists uncovering new medicines or astronauts exploring the mysteries of space. In schools, pupils are often tasked with 'researching' topics such as how plants grow or the traditions of ancient civilisations. However, the ubiquity of its usage means that defining exactly what the word research means is somewhat challenging.

> **ACTION LEARNING SET**
>
> Reflective Question
>
> Think about activities you engage with in your daily lives that you would badge as being research. How do they relate to the form definitions as presented in the Frascati Manual, a document that is designed to standardise methodologies for collecting formal research and development data across Europe?
>
> - Basic research is experimental or theoretical work undertaken primarily to acquire new knowledge of the underlying foundations of phenomena and observable facts, without any particular application or use in view.
> - Applied research is original investigation undertaken in order to acquire new knowledge. It is, however, directed primarily towards a specific, practical aim or objective (OECD, 2015).
>
> To help explain how research will be viewed in this chapter, Clough and Nutbrown (2012) outline three criteria that allow formal research to be distinguished from other 'finding-out' type activities.

1. Research is purposive; it is the creation of knowledge to solve a problem, answer a question or better describe or understand something.
2. Research is positional; it is undertaken by people, in a specific context, and only becomes research when it is shared with others.
3. Research is political in that it should be intended to make a difference and to bring about change.

As Murdoch (2023) notes, research should also be understood as part of a continuous cycle, reflecting its iterative and dynamic nature. Researchers revisit, refine, and adapt their approaches to inquiry in response to emerging insights, challenges, and evolving questions. This ensures the deepening of understanding and the production of meaningful, contextually relevant knowledge. The core principles of this cycle are outlined in Fig. 7.1.

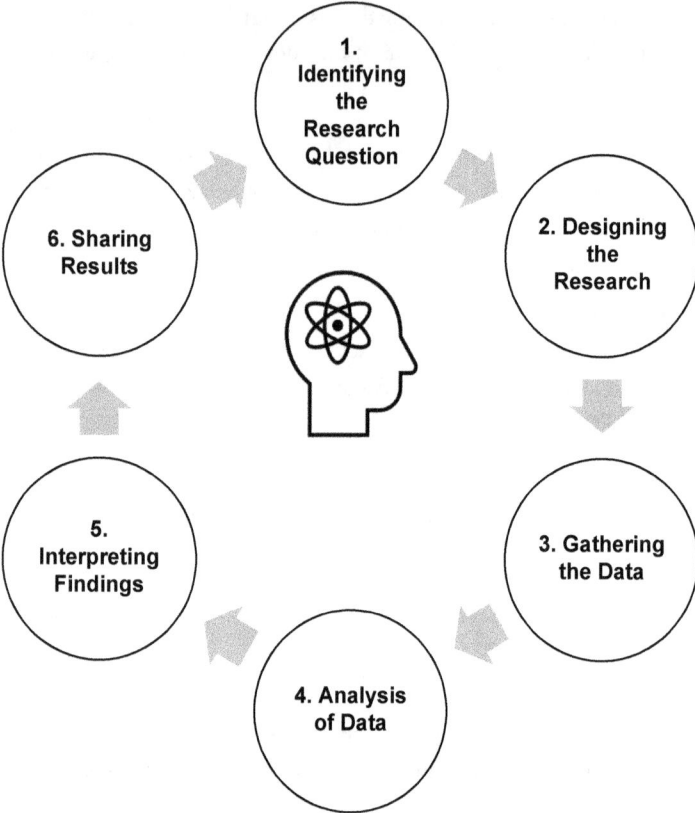

Fig. 7.1. The Cycle of Research.

However, when thinking about research with pupils, our understanding of research extends beyond formal scientific or academic practices. It is rather about cultivating curiosity, engaging actively with the world around them, making connections, and developing new understandings. Kellett (2005) highlights that such research practices represent the emergence of a new research paradigm that challenges traditional, adult-dominated approaches to knowledge. This paradigm emphasises pupils' autonomy and agency and recognises their capacity to generate meaningful insights and knowledge. As Murdoch (2023) finds, the cyclical nature of research aligns with the way pupils engage in independent learning in that it is driven by their innate curiosity about the world. The end point of this process is different from where the cycle began.

WHY SHOULD PUPILS BE RESEARCHERS?

More than three decades after the United Nations Convention on the Rights of the Child (UNCRC) was adopted by the UN General Assembly in 1989, the human rights of pupils have become increasingly central to policymaking (Fielding & Bragg, 2003). These rights have shaped political and social practices and influenced how knowledge about children and childhood is produced. A cornerstone of this framework is Article 12 of the UNCRC, which asserts that children capable of forming their own views have the right to express them freely in all matters affecting them (UNICEF, 1989). Engaging pupils in research brings this principle to life, offering them the chance to explore questions that matter most to them. It validates their personal perspectives, boosts self-esteem, and underscores their ability to contribute to meaningful societal change. Crucially, it amplifies their voices, drawing on the unique insights shaped by their lived experiences. For the teacher, this can deepen our understanding of their worlds, revealing perspectives and solutions that might otherwise remain hidden.

At the outset, it is crucial to distinguish between research that is conducted *with* pupils and research conducted *by* pupils. These two approaches can be seen to occupy opposite ends of a spectrum, as depicted in Fig. 7.2.

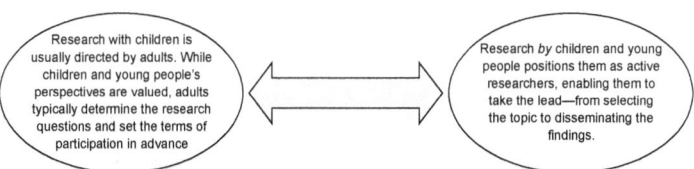

Fig. 7.2. Research with and By Pupils.

> **REFLECTIVE QUESTION**
>
> Consider where you would place the following examples on the continuum above and why that might be.
>
> - **Example 1:** A group of 10-year-olds decide that they want to conduct research on playground inclusivity. With initial training from adults in basic research methods, the pupils set their research agenda, choosing to explore how welcoming the playground is for students of different abilities. They design surveys, conduct interviews, and observe their peers, using methods that feel meaningful and manageable for them. After analysing their findings, the pupils present their insights to the school community. Throughout the process, adults act as facilitators, offering guidance and resources while allowing the pupils to take the lead.
>
> - **Example 2:** A Year 2 class begins a project exploring students' feelings about homework. Adults and pupils co-construct the research agenda, collaboratively developing questions about how homework affects their daily lives and wellbeing. Together, they decide on methods such as group discussions, drawings, and short questionnaires to collect data. The pupils actively participate as both researchers, leading discussions and gathering responses, and participants, sharing their own experiences. Some pupils also contribute to analysing and presenting the findings at a school assembly.

These two examples also align with the work of Bakhtiar et al. (2023), who highlight the different approaches that can be taken when engaging pupils in research. They use the following terminology to explain the different approaches that you might take in your classrooms or settings.

- **Pupil-Led Research:** As outlined in example 1 above. This approach places pupils at the centre of the research process, positioning them as the primary decision-makers while adults take on a supportive role as facilitators. It acknowledges pupils' capacity to lead inquiries into topics that are important to them, empowering them to take full ownership of the research from inception to completion.

- **Co-researcher Model:** As outlined in example 2 above. In this model, pupils and adults form a collaborative partnership, sharing responsibilities for planning, conducting, and interpreting research. The co-researcher model strikes a balanced 'middle ground'. Pupils are actively involved in decision-making and execution, while adults offer guidance and expertise as needed. This approach ensures that pupils' voices and ideas are central while creating a supportive and inclusive environment for truly collaborative research outcomes.

ETHICAL CONSIDERATIONS

Holzscheiter et al. (2019) argue that while the UNCRC has been pivotal in emphasising the importance of children's voices, it has also, perhaps inadvertently, contributed to the regulation and control of their experiences. For example, initiatives such as school councils, while intended to amplify the voices of pupils, often operate within the boundaries of adult-led agendas, restricting the genuine influence that pupil participants can have. The seminal work of Hart (1992) provides a useful framework for understanding this dynamic, using the metaphor of a ladder to depict the varying levels of pupils' participation in decision-making. These levels range from tokenistic involvement, where pupils have little real agency, to genuine collaboration and empowerment, where their contributions are meaningful and impactful. Similarly, Spriggs and Gillam (2017) highlight the transformative potential of engaging pupils in research but also stress the need for the teacher to recognise the significant ethical challenges that such engagement entails.

The work of Cowie and Khoo (2017) provides a framework which is designed to support co-research with pupils. This is structured around three key principles: access, authenticity, and advocacy.

Access

Researchers must ensure that all pupils have opportunities to participate in the research and that they are adequately supported in doing so. This involves identifying the skills and competencies pupils may need and providing the resources and time necessary to develop them. Researchers should critically reflect on their own power within the research process and consider how to create equitable opportunities for participation.

Authenticity

Authenticity requires researchers to genuinely listen to pupils' perspectives and ensure their voices are central to the research. Strategies might include co-creating research questions with pupils, allowing them to lead parts of the process, and using child-friendly methods like drawings, storytelling, or digital tools to enable them to express their ideas fully. The goal is to honour pupils' contributions and avoid tokenistic involvement.

Advocacy

Advocacy focuses on ensuring pupils benefit from the research process and view their participation as meaningful. This involves identifying how their involvement can shape outcomes, such as influencing policy, improving practices, or addressing issues they prioritise. Engaging pupils as researchers also enhances the validity of research by fostering a shared understanding of questions and dilemmas and by providing richer insights into the perspective of the pupils.

CASE STUDY

Ethical Considerations in Action

In this example, a Year 2 class at a primary school conducted a research project to investigate their favourite playground activities of their peers. The project was structured with a clear goal: to empower the pupils by actively involving them as researchers, providing them with a platform to share their perspectives, and ensuring their insights could drive meaningful improvements to their play environment.

Access in Action

The project began with interactive workshops designed to introduce the basics of research. These sessions were tailored to the needs of the pupils. They learned and practised foundational skills such as observing others, asking questions, and recording information using symbols or drawings. Ensuring access for all was a priority, and alternative methods, such as drawing or storytelling, were used to help all pupils share their ideas. For those with additional needs, tools like communication boards, visual aids, and one-on-one support from teaching assistants ensured their voices were heard. Throughout the process, the teacher-researcher reflected on their role, acting as a guide rather than a leader.

Authenticity in Action

The pupils played an active role in shaping the research from start to finish, ensuring authenticity was central to the process. In a group discussion, they created research questions such as *'What games do children like the most?'* and *'Why do some children not join in?'* and voted on which one they would use. To collect data, they selected three methods: observation, where groups recorded playground activities using clipboards; interviews, where pairs asked classmates simple questions like, *'What's your favourite game, and why?'*; and creative expression, where pupils drew pictures of their favourite playground moments and shared these in small groups. They created a colourful chart to showcase activity preferences and a poster summarising their observations.

Advocacy in Action

Advocacy was a critical part of the project, ensuring that the pupils' contributions led to meaningful outcomes. The pupils reflected on their findings and proposed ways to improve their playground experience. For example, when many pupils expressed a desire for more creative play options, the group presented their suggestions to senior leaders, with the teacher-researcher facilitating the process while keeping the pupils' voices central. Their findings prompted practical changes, such

> as adding new play equipment, introducing structured activities for pupils who felt left out, and creating a buddy system to support social inclusion. By the end of the project, the pupils saw how their contributions had led to tangible improvements, reinforcing the importance of their voices and ideas, with one proudly stating, '*It feels good that we helped make the playground better for everyone*'.

CREATING AN APPROPRIATE RESEARCH QUESTION

The foundation of any research lies in developing a strong research question. While this might seem to be straightforward, identifying the right question is often more challenging than it first appears. For teachers aiming to support their pupils' engagement in research, establishing a climate of inquiry in their classroom should be the essential first step. In doing this, Salmon and Barrera (2021) call upon the teacher to build upon the interests, lived experiences and previous learning of the pupils.

Activities that we have seen as we have visited classrooms have included the following.

- **'What If' Scenarios:** Use imaginative prompts like '*What if animals could talk?*' or '*What if we had no electricity for a week?*' to inspire creative and investigable questions.

- **Storytelling as a Prompt:** Read a book or share a story and invite pupils to develop questions about the characters, setting, or plot. For example, after reading about a scientist in a storybook, pupils might ask, 'What experiments could we try to replicate what they discovered?'

- **Daily Wonder Time:** Dedicate a few minutes each day for pupils to share something they've wondered about during lessons or activities. For example, after a science experiment, a pupil might ask, '*What would happen if we tried this with a different material?*'

- **Contrasts and Comparisons:** Encourage pupils to compare two things they encounter in their lives or learning. For example,

'Why do cats and dogs behave differently?' or *'What makes stories in books different from movies?'*

Philosophy for Children (P4C) is another educational approach designed to encourage critical, creative, and collaborative thinking among young learners that can be used to establish a climate of inquiry in your classroom. P4C creates opportunities for pupils to explore big ideas, question assumptions, and engage in meaningful dialogue. At the heart of P4C is the Community of Inquiry, where pupils and teachers come together to discuss philosophical questions sparked by a shared stimulus, such as a story, picture, or real-life scenario. The process begins with pupils identifying and posing questions inspired by the stimulus, such as *'What is fairness?'* or *'Can something be real if we can't see it?'* The group then selects a question to explore collectively, with the teacher acting as a facilitator rather than an instructor. To find out more about this approach and to access resources and training, you should refer to the SAPERE (n.d.) (https://www.sapere.org.uk), which is the national charity for P4C, Communities and Colleges.

However, it is also crucial for teachers to recognise that, in the context of inquiry, not all questions hold the same value or potential for meaningful exploration.

REFLECTIVE QUESTIONS

Consider the questions listed below that have been prepared by pupils. Evaluate them, considering their quality and the possibilities they offer for research.

- What types of games do pupils enjoy most during playtime?
- What factors make a book popular in our class?
- What materials are best for building the strongest bridge in our science experiment?
- Do kids like playtime?
- How do we solve global warming?

A well-crafted research question is essential for meaningful inquiry and should adhere to several key principles. Specificity is crucial, as clear and manageable topics (e.g., '*What types of games are most popular in our class?*' rather than '*What do pupils like?*') provide focus and direction. Questions should also be open-ended, encouraging exploration and critical thinking (e.g., '*How do pupils choose their favourite playground games?*' instead of '*Do pupils like football?*'). Additionally, questions must be age-appropriate, aligning with the pupils' understanding and capabilities (e.g., '*What makes a story exciting to read?*' rather than '*How does narrative structure influence reader engagement?*'). Finally, feasibility is key; the question should be realistic to investigate within the available resources and timeframe, ensuring the research process is both achievable and engaging.

A RESEARCH METHODS TOOLBOX

Once you have identified the right research question, the next step is supporting your pupils in selecting the most appropriate method to use in their investigation (Johnson et al., 2014). Conducting research is akin to tackling a DIY project, which requires that you carefully choose the right tools for each task. For example, you would be unlikely to try to hammer a nail in with a screwdriver. Similarly, pupils need to understand that they need to make choices from the different approaches or methods, picking the one that will be best to answer their research question. Some possible approaches that we have seen in schools are outlined below, and the toolkit provided by Johnson et al. (2014) also provides a comprehensive overview of how these might be implemented in your classroom or setting.

CREATIVE AND EXPRESSIVE METHODS

These provide pupils with diverse and engaging ways to explore and communicate their thoughts, experiences, and ideas. Drawing and mapping can allow them to visualise complex emotions or spatial relationships, offering insights into how they perceive their environments. Photography enables them to document their surroundings and daily life, capturing unique perspectives and moments that might otherwise be overlooked. Collage or scrapbooking allows them to assemble visual and textual elements into a cohesive representation of their ideas.

INTERACTIVE AND PARTICIPATORY METHODS

These methods draw upon collaboration and dialogue. Through conducting interviews, pupils can pose questions to peers, adults, or experts. Focus groups provide a platform for small group discussions, allowing participants to share and refine ideas collectively. Surveys and questionnaires offer a structured approach for pupils to gather data systematically, helping them understand patterns and trends. Peer observations enable pupils to study behaviours and activities in their social environment.

DIGITAL AND TECHNOLOGY-BASED METHODS

Digital storytelling allows pupils to craft narratives using multimedia tools, blending text, images, sound, and video to create dynamic, engaging accounts of their lived experiences. Video recording enables pupils to capture events or present findings in a visual format, enhancing their ability to document and communicate effectively. Audio diaries provide a platform for recording spoken reflections and observations, offering an intimate and immediate way to capture thoughts and emotions.

SENSORY AND EXPERIENTIAL METHODS

These immerse pupils in the research process by engaging their senses and lived experiences. Walk-alongs or tours allow pupils to reflect on specific environments as they move through them, offering real-time insights into their perceptions and interactions. Sensory mapping captures the smells, sounds, textures, and sights of a given area, providing a rich, multi-dimensional understanding of the environment. Play-based research uses guided or free play as a medium for exploration, enabling pupils to express their ideas and discover new concepts naturally and intuitively.

TEXT-BASED AND ANALYTICAL METHODS

These provide pupils with structured and reflective approaches to research, encouraging critical thinking and organisation. Journaling allows them to record thoughts, feelings, and observations over time, fostering self-awareness and providing a rich, personal account of their experiences. Content analysis enables pupils to delve into books, media, or other materials, developing their ability to identify themes, patterns, and meanings. Mind mapping offers a visual way to structure ideas and explore relationships between concepts, helping pupils to organise their thoughts and see connections more clearly.

PROBLEM-SOLVING AND EXPERIMENTAL METHODS

Conducting experiments allows them to test hypotheses and explore phenomena through structured activities, helping them understand cause-and-effect relationships. Design challenges encourage pupils to create prototypes to address specific issues, promoting practical problem-solving skills.

ARTISTIC AND PERFORMANCE-BASED METHODS

These provide pupils with creative outlets to explore and express their ideas. Music and dance enable pupils to convey emotions and concepts through movement and sound, offering a powerful, non-verbal form of communication. Theatre and puppetry allow pupils to use performance to explore scenarios, develop narratives, and share insights in a visually compelling manner. Creating murals gives pupils the opportunity to visually depict their research findings, transforming abstract ideas into tangible, impactful artworks.

PROVIDING APPROPRIATE SCAFFOLDING AND SUPPORT

While pupils' agency is central to collaborative research, the role of teachers and facilitators is equally critical in providing guidance and support. Striking the right balance requires careful scaffolding that empowers pupils to take the lead while also ensuring they have the tools and frameworks necessary to succeed. Navigating this balance requires the teacher to be highly reflexive about the extent to which their perspective is present in the research process and also the way findings and results are presented (Kim, 2016).

Questions you could ask yourself might include:

- How do my own beliefs, experiences, and values shape the way I guide the research process?

- How do I ensure that the power dynamic between myself and the pupils does not limit their ability to lead and contribute authentically?

- How do I create opportunities for pupils to explore their own interests and ideas without overwhelming them with too much freedom or too many restrictions?

- Whose voices are most prominent in the presentation of findings? Is it truly reflective of the pupils' contributions?

- Are all pupils' voices being heard, or are certain individuals or groups dominating the process?

- How do I navigate situations where the pupils' choices or findings may conflict with my own professional or ethical judgement?

Greig et al. (2012) write that a strong starting point for any research project is to guide pupils in analysing existing research conducted by their peers. Encourage them to examine the methods used, discuss why those approaches were chosen, and reflect on how they contributed to answering the overarching research question. The creation of age-appropriate research guides can also help demystify the research process by providing clear, manageable steps for pupils to follow. These guides can include practical examples, tips for organising their ideas, and tools to support their chosen methods, such as templates for recording observations or frameworks for analysing data. By breaking down the process into accessible stages, you can empower pupils to approach their research with confidence and curiosity, fostering a deeper engagement with the inquiry process.

> **ACTION LEARNING SET**
>
> Before beginning to engage pupils in inquiry, you may wish to engage in the following:
> - How can you support pupils who may require more support with formulating questions or organising their ideas?
> - What guided questions might be used to provoke thinking and probe understanding?
> - How could teachers encourage pupils to be reflexive about their decisions, methods, and findings, understand what worked, what could be improved, and how they can apply their learning to future projects?

It is also essential to reflect on the effect this has on you as an educator. Consider keeping a professional journal to capture your experiences, documenting successes, challenges, and the lessons you've learned along the way. This will allow you to identify areas where you can improve, celebrate moments of breakthrough, and develop a deeper awareness of how your role evolves when pupils take the lead (Kim, 2016). However, it is also important to acknowledge that this can challenge traditional power dynamics in the classroom, prompting you to critically evaluate your role in decision-making in your classroom. As we have found, this shift can be both empowering and humbling, requiring you to trust your pupils and come to embrace a more flexible and responsive approach across all your teaching practices.

CONCLUSION

In conclusion, this chapter has demonstrated how inquiry-based learning strategies enable teachers to empower pupils to actively engage in meaningful exploration. We have shown that cultivating a culture of inquiry in the classroom starts with nurturing curiosity and embedding critical thinking into everyday teaching practices. We highlighted the importance of careful ethical considerations, which form the foundation of any research process, ensuring that pupils' voices are respected and their contributions are meaningful. Building upon this foundation, the different methods that might be used to support research were outlined, and we considered how these might be scaffolded by the teacher. Throughout this chapter, we have highlighted the crucial role of teacher reflexivity in the research process. We emphasised the need for you to critically evaluate your role as a guide and facilitator, ensuring your involvement does not inadvertently reinforce power dynamics that could limit the agency or authenticity of the pupils who are involved.

> **REVIEW OF CHAPTER OBJECTIVES**
>
> In this chapter, you have
>
> - Consider what is meant by conducting research *with* pupils and explore its significance in fostering their confidence and agency.
>
> - Examine the ethical implications that must be addressed before initiating any research project.
>
> - Reflect on what constitutes an appropriate research question and discover methods that pupils can use to investigate and reach conclusions.
>
> - Investigate how teachers can scaffold pupils' explorations without imposing or dominating their process.

FURTHER READING

Johnson, V., Hart, R., & Colwell. (2014). *Steps to engaging young children in research*. University of Brighton.

Kellett, M. (2005). *How to develop children as researchers: A step by step guide to teaching the research process*. SAGE Publications.

Kim, C., Sheehy, K., & Kerawalla, L. (2017). *Developing children as researchers: A practical guide to help children conduct social research*. Taylor & Francis.

SAPERE. (n.d.). *SAPERE philosophy for children and communities*. SAPERE. Retrieved January 9, 2025, from https://www.sapere.org.uk/

REFERENCES

Bakhtiar, A., Lang, M., Shelley, B., & West, M. (2023). Research with and by children: A systematic literature review. *Review of Education, 11*(1), e3384. https://doi.org/10.1002/rev3.3384

Clough, P., & Nutbrown, C. (2012). *A student's guide to methodology* (3rd ed.). Sage Publications Ltd.

Cowie, B., & Khoo, E. (2017). Accountability through access, authenticity and advocacy when researching with young children. *International Journal of Inclusive Education, 21*, 1–14. https://doi.org/10.1080/13603116.2016.1260821

Fielding, M., & Bragg, S. (2003). *Students as researchers: Making a difference*. Pearson Publishing.

Greig, A. D., Taylor, J., & MacKay, T. (2012). *Doing research with children: A practical guide*. SAGE Publications. https://books.google.co.uk/books?id=zTb7AwAAQBAJ

Hart, R. (1992). *Children's participation: From tokenism to citizenship*. Innocenti Essays. Vol. 4. United Nations Children's Fund.

Holzscheiter, A., Josefsson, J., & Sandin, B. (2019). Child rights governance: An introduction. *Childhood, 26*(3), 271–288. https://doi.org/10.1177/0907568219854518

Johnson, V., Hart, R., & Colwell, J. (2014). *Steps to engaging young children in research*. University of Brighton.

Kim, C.-Y. (2016). Why research 'by' children? Rethinking the assumptions underlying the facilitation of children as researchers. *Children & Society, 30*(3), 230–240. https://doi.org/10.1111/chso.12133

Murdoch, K. (2023). *From agency to zest: A journey through the landscape of inquiry*. Elevate Books EDU.

OECD. (2015). *Frascati manual 2015: Guidelines for collecting and reporting data on research and experimental development*. OECD. https://doi.org/10.1787/9789264239012-en

Salmon, A., & Barrera, M. (2021). Intentional questioning to promote thinking and learning. *Thinking Skills and Creativity*, *40*, 100822. https://doi.org/10.1016/j.tsc.2021.100822

SAPERE. (n.d.). *SAPERE philosophy for children and communities*. SAPERE. Retrieved January 9, 2025, from https://www.sapere.org.uk/

Spriggs, M., & Gillam, L. (2017). Ethical complexities in child co-research. *Research Ethics*, *15*(1), 1–16. https://doi.org/10.1177/1747016117750207

UNICEF. (1989). *United Nations convention on the rights of the child*. https://www.unicef.org.uk/what-we-do/un-convention-child-rights/

8

WHAT IS EVIDENCE-BASED PRACTICE, AND (HOW) DOES IT WORK IN EDUCATION?

Ed Podesta

Leeds Trinity University, UK

CHAPTER OBJECTIVES

By the end of this chapter, readers should be able to:

- **Explain what educational research is** and how it relates to teaching, learning, and policy.
- **Understand the development and critique of evidence-based education (EBE)**, especially in comparison to evidence-based medicine (EBM).
- **Identify and reflect on the various ways teachers can use research** in their professional practice (instrumental, symbolic, and conceptual).
- **Consider the importance of teacher judgement and context** in applying research, and explore broader, pragmatic definitions of research in education.

Keywords: Educational research; evidence based education (EBE); research use in education; teacher professional development; research practice gap; education policy; educational methodology; teaching and learning; curriculum and pedagogy; discipline of education

INTRODUCTION

We often think of research as a highly technical activity, perhaps based on statistical evidence of the impact of specific interventions – techniques, treatments or medicines. Some policymakers, teachers and school leaders have promoted the idea of Evidence Based Practice 'EBE' based on this notion of research. They have also used the practice of medicine as an example of a profession that has dramatically improved through the better use of research.

After considering the advantages and disadvantages, for education and teaching, of looking at research in this way, we will argue for a broader approach. The argument will outline different ways of using research and the way that different interests might influence it. We will close by proposing that thinking of the study of 'education' as an ongoing conversation between parents, teachers, pupils, policy makers and wider society, as well as researchers, might increasingly be necessary to help us understand and improve education in the context of living in a democracy.

CRITICISM OF EDUCATIONAL RESEARCH

Long-held political and professional frustrations about the quality of educational research and of educational researchers are clear from key speeches and interventions made in recent decades (Hall, 2023). Philpott and Poultney (2025) point out that educational research has been criticised for failing to provide cumulative bodies of knowledge (Hargreaves, 2007), for not producing enough research that policy makers could use to make generalised predictions about effectiveness (Blunkett, 2000, p. 200), for the use of flimsy methodologies based on vague 'buzzword terminology' (Gorard & Torgerson, 2006) and, more recently, for failing to take advantage of key developments in research methods (Goldacre, 2013). Throughout this criticism is an underlying comparison between education and medicine, which is presented as a practice which has taken advantage of scientific evidence (Slavin, 2002).

Influential educators and edu-entrepreneurs have allied with policy makers in recent years (Craske, 2021) and arguably the criticism has taken an accelerated and more aggressive form; presenting educational academics and researchers as regressive ideologues (Gove, 2013, p. 12), determined to hold onto influence by refusing to admit to the efficacy of learning science (Severs, 2022) or what others have called 'what works' (Biesta, 2007). In terms that sometimes approach allegations of conspiracy, it was argued that teachers have been kept in the dark.

Overall, the argument was that scientific knowledge about teaching, based on real research, should be given to teachers so that they can take a great 'leap forward' (Goldacre, 2013) into a world of effective, 'EBE'. As we will see, it is important to note that this argument was sometimes promoted in divisive ways that dismissed the 'hot mess' (Jones, 2023) of teaching based on tradition, personal should be personal advantage, or ideology (Collins, 2018a, 2018b), and compared it to evidence-informed practice that embraced the science of 'what works'.

In England, since 2010, there has been an explosion of research, blogs, books, and other publications which have sought to break through such 'gatekeeping'. A series of reforms proposed a 'golden thread' between teacher training and post-qualification development, based on specific 'evidence-based' pedagogic techniques (Hordern & Brooks, 2023, 2024). The then Conservative-led coalition government sponsored a 'grassroots' research movement under the banner of ResearchEd, and created institutions such as the Educational Endowment Foundation (EEF). The EEF was designed to collate syntheses and meta-syntheses of evidence in order to promote the use of 'what works' techniques (Edovald & Nevill, 2021).

THE BEST KIND OF EVIDENCE? SCIENCE AND 'THE FAIR TEST'

Research findings based on large-scale research of quantitative (number based) evidence are popular with policymakers because they offer recommendations that seem as if they can be generalised and applied across large populations (Blunkett, 2000). Their appeal also draws on popular ideas of what research and science should be like – that it should lead to truth (Mason-Wilkes, 2018), cures and breakthroughs, just as we hope medicine will (Durant et al., 1992; Wrigley & McCusker, 2019). This can make it very difficult for researchers to talk about risks, chances, uncertainties and areas of doubt (van der Bles et al., 2019) and, as we will see, it could have important implications for the relationship between educational research and educational practice.

'Scientific' research like this is based on ideas such as the 'fair test' and the 'controlled trial', that is, a kind of experiment that allows for comparisons between different types of 'treatment', in situations that are as similar to each other as possible. Researchers want to be sure that they are comparing the 'independent variables' (the different kinds of treatment) and keeping all the other variables the same, or 'controlled' as much as possible (Clarke & Ravindran, 2019). This is most often done by giving the new treatment to the 'intervention group' and comparing the outcomes to the 'control' group, which does not receive the treatment (or gets the usual treatment). Statistical methods and tests can then be used to understand whether there are patterns of outcomes which can tell us whether the treatment is effective or not (Coe et al., 2021). The interpretation of these results is then often communicated on the basis of 'effect sizes', 'sample size' and 'statistical significance', and when applied to practice, often with an underlying assumption that bigger is better (Didau, 2014).

It is important for researchers to make sure that the control group and intervention group are as similar as possible. Otherwise, differences between them might cause 'bias' in outcomes. To avoid this risk, researchers use a method called 'Randomised Controlled Trials' (RTCs). RTCs use a random method of allocating people taking part in the trial to either the treatment group or the control group. The theory behind this random allocation has it that any differences between these groups will be averaged out by the randomness of the chance of ending up in either group – so that an effect observed in the data are more likely to be caused by the treatment than any statistical accident in the makeup of the groups (Sullivan, 2011).

Similar attention has been given to the use of meta-analysis, or systematic reviews in education (Pirrie, 2001; Wiliam, 2019). These use statistical tools and methods to combine the findings of several different studies about a technique, intervention or treatment in order to answer questions about their impact, effectiveness (or otherwise) (Page et al., 2014).

Coe (2002) suggests that the validity and strengths of claims arising from meta-analysis and systematic reviews are directly related to the extent to which the studies they include as evidence are 'high quality', and well-matched to each other:

- They should have similar outcome measures.
- Their outcome measures should derive from similar instruments.
- They should compare similar populations.
- They should compare similar interventions, treatments or techniques, not just interventions with similar labels or names.

EBM has used systematic reviews in order to create robust information about the efficacy of techniques based on a broad foundation of evidence, and so that this synthesis of evidence can be presented to practitioners (Sackett et al., 1996). Their use in Education has also been promoted, and some very famous studies have had a very important influence on practice and policy (Davies, 1999; Hattie, 2008).

EVIDENCE-BASED MEDICINE (EBM)

As we have seen, policy makers looked to medicine as a good example of an improved 'Evidence Based' profession (Goldacre, 2013; Hargreaves, 1994), and argued that education could also become a more effective, by following that example. To understand this claim, we need to consider how EBM has developed and whether the example has been carefully considered or applied to education.

The Purpose of EBM

In the 1990s and early 2000s groups of medics and medical educators in Canada, the US, and Europe successfully collaborated over the development of training programmes which were designed to teach doctors how to understand the quality and validity of research claims, and how to use the resulting high-quality evidence in clinical decision-making – deciding on the treatment and care of patients. This movement became known as EBM (Claridge & Fabian, 2005; Sur & Dahm, 2011).

The early emphasis of this movement was on educating medical practitioners about research evidence of the impact of specific techniques, ways of evaluating the quality of that evidence, and procedures that allowed them to take the evidence into account in their professional decision-making (Djulbegovic & Guyatt, 2017). This has led to a focus on producing syntheses of research, alongside guidelines for standardised processes and treatments based on high quality research evidence (Fernandez et al., 2015; Sur & Dahm, 2011). EBM has also consistently focused on the way that doctors use research evidence in their practice (Greenhalgh, 2014b). This focus on doctors' judgement is fundamental aspect of the EBM movement (Sackett et al., 1996), which recognises this as a 'complex process of clinical decision-making – which includes data gathering, years of medical knowledge, experience, and astute intuition' (Sur & Dahm, 2011). The aim was therefore to enhance rather than replace clinical judgement; to improve decisions about the appropriateness of a particular treatment or technique.

Debate About EBM in the Medical Profession

Even so, doctors worried that EBM might become overly 'algorithmic' (Sur & Dahm, 2011) and take decision-making, agency and autonomy away from clinicians and patients (Fernandez et al., 2015). This led to fears that restricting doctor's judgements and the treatments at their disposal to only those seen as reflecting 'the best evidence', could cause decisions that are not in patients' interests, or that do not recognise their particular contexts, values (Claridge & Fabian, 2005; Mykhalovskiy & Weir, 2004; Renedo et al., 2018) or even the range of overlapping illnesses and issues which patients experience in real-world situations (Greenhalgh, 2014a; McKnight & Morgan, 2023).

Increasingly, the EBM movement also recognised that the labelling particular forms of research as 'best available evidence', such as RCTs, might mean that important research with other formats would be ignored (Blunt, 2015). Doctors wanted different kinds of study designs (such as case studies, observational studies, qualitative studies about experiences and values) to be recognised as having a role in research and practice of medicine (Edwards et al., 2004).

These debates also allowed for increased awareness of the role of political and private commercial interests which can cause bias and errors (Goldenberg, 2006) by promoting or even falsifying 'evidence' which brings them profit and influence (Greenhalgh et al., 2014a). These interests can also marginalise practice that does not conform to this 'evidence' (Djulbegovic & Guyatt, 2017). For instance, new products are more likely to get promoted than unfashionable (but more effective) treatments by crucial influencers (Greenhalgh, 2014b, p. 203).

> **BIAS IN RANDOMISED CONTROLLED TRIALS**
>
> - Patient selection – studies that use participants who have a high baseline risk show higher levels of impact (Hegedus & Moody, 2010).
>
> - Comparator selection – studies that choose weak comparators, or which enact comparator treatments in less effective ways, increase effect size (Mann & Djulbegovic, 2013).
>
> - Faulty inclusion criteria – research syntheses which include poor-quality research or that group together inappropriately different studies when attempting to calculate effect sizes in systematic reviews or meta-syntheses can inflate effect sizes (Page et al., 2014).
>
> A good example of the way that promoted 'evidence' can obscure important 'evidence' is the 'File Drawer Effect'. This

form of 'publication bias' refers to the way that inconvenient or commercially uninteresting research ends up hidden in desk drawers rather than being published. Research usually only gets published if it shows positive effects of a treatment or intervention – so we never get to read about (the much greater amount of) research which 'failed' to show an effect (Arquero, 2023; Hardwicke & Wagenmakers, 2023).

'FILE DRAW EFFECT'

This publication bias means that it is very hard for researchers to find out about research that:

- Challenges accepted (or profitable) treatments and techniques.

- Highlights the contexts, practices or other factors which mean that otherwise 'effective' techniques are more likely or less likely to work.

- Helps other researchers decide what research they should undertake, or even avoid, on the grounds that other people have already done it.

THE LESSONS OF EBM

Debate and Dialogue Between Research and Practice in Medicine

Overall, we can see that EBM has responded to the challenges that practitioners and commentators have raised (Sackett et al., 1996). Collaboration (often international) between researchers and practitioners was a key characteristic of the EBM approach (Fernandez et al., 2015). Developing a common vocabulary for EBM enabled the profession to communicate concepts of bias, reliability, quality and application, rather than only delineating or even requiring specific practices. And, in debating these concerns, practitioners and researchers have improved standards for clinical research together (Djulbegovic & Guyatt, 2017).

Different Evidence, Different Expertise

The EBM movement, therefore, continues to recognise the difference between 'expert knowledge' and 'expert opinion', and the way that different kinds of evidence can help us understand effectiveness in a trial population and in the context of the patient (Fernandez et al., 2015). We might want to call these different kinds of research:

- Explanatory – 'proof of concept', designed to find out whether a technique or treatment will work in ideal or 'lab' conditions.
- Pragmatic – which investigates whether a technique or treatment works in 'real world' settings and also whether such a technique is 'worth it', taking into account the effect and the various costs and resources involved (Djulbegovic & Guyatt, 2017).

This recognition of different kinds of evidence and expertise in turn makes it possible for practitioners to continue to make judgements about the different kinds of benefits and costs. They can also take the patient's views into account. One could argue that there has been an iterative relationship between EBM and its critics. The latter has set progressive challenges, which proponents of EBM have responded to by developing increasingly sophisticated processes and concepts to address them.

CASE STUDY – DIFFERENT USES OF RESEARCH IN EDUCATION POLICY AND PRACTICE

Having considered the meaning and development of EBM, it might be helpful to consider the different ways that you have encountered and used research about teaching in your training and continuing development. This case study outlines some ways of thinking about the use of research.

Cain and Allan (2017) did some interesting research looking at the different ways in which research gets used:

- Instrumental uses – where research is applied to practice, in ways that make it concrete and usable for practitioners.

- Symbolic uses – as a tool of persuasion, or for political purposes or other ways of legitimising policy, practice or even a lack of policy.

- Conceptual uses – as a resource to change the way that we think, which might (or might not) develop into or through practice.

Reflective Questions

- Do you tend to encounter research that someone else has found, or do you find research by making your own searches?

- What kinds of research uses do you most often experience (Instrumental – to help with specific problems, Symbolic – to persuade you to act in certain ways, or Conceptual, as a resource to help you think)?

- Do you have particular key pieces of research that you refer to often? What kind of things does it help you with, are these pragmatic, explanatory, or other kinds of research?

(RE)EVALUATING THE IDEA OF EBE

You'll recall that the main criticisms of educational research are firstly, it has not made enough impact on teachers' practice and pupils' outcomes, and secondly, this failure of impact has been caused by educational researchers' refusal or inability to consistently build knowledge using scientific methods of inquiry and evidence. As this next section will argue, this is a very limited, narrow, and partial consideration of the problem.

In fact, many of the important aspects of the research-practice gap outlined above in relation to medicine are imagined away by those promoting the approach in teaching. We have allowed policymakers and interested parties to define a very narrow and politicised problem in education (Pirrie, 2001), with a focus on only one aspect – getting research-based techniques enacted with fidelity in the classroom.

Challenges to EBE

Just as with EBM, researchers and practitioners have challenged aspects of EBE. However, the response of policymakers and some researchers has made it difficult for EBE to benefit from this debate and challenge in the same way medicine has.

Some of the key criticisms of the 'what works' movement in education arise from the way that it has used 'evidence'. The difficulty of applying findings from controlled environments, where all other variables are limited, to real-world situations (Sullivan, 2011; Wiliam, 2019) means this kind of research can only get us so far, because it only tells us what *has* worked in the (often quite restricted) conditions under which the research was done (Stenhouse, 1981). Education takes place in an extremely 'open' system in which intervening events, attitudes, causes, lives and personal histories constantly interact (Wrigley & McCusker, 2019).

Biesta goes even further in arguing that education is not like medicine, in that 'being a student is not an illness, just as teaching is not a cure' (Biesta, 2007, p. 33) and that teaching is not subject to 'cause and effect'. Teaching relies much more on the interaction between human minds using symbolic meanings. These interactions between teachers and students, and between students themselves, are the means by which pupils learn, and they learn about things from the ways that we teach them as much as the content that is taught (Biesta, 2007, 2013).

The problem of assuming that 'scientific' evidence will produce reliable prescriptions of 'what works' is magnified with the use of systematic reviews and meta-syntheses of research, which need care to be taken when selecting studies for inclusion, and when deciding how and what to compare when calculating effect sizes. One of the most influential pieces of research on 'what works', John Hattie's *Visible Learning* has come under intense critique, and even been described as 'pseudoscience' (Bergeron & Rivard, 2017). This is because it seems to combine studies without considering the different ages of participants, lengths of intervention, differences between 'controlled' comparisons and 'before and after' comparisons, different outcomes (for instance mixing studies about impact on things as different as 'self esteem', 'attainment', 'achievement of graduation'), ignoring accepted standards for research synthesis (Wrigley & McCusker, 2019).

Research which only focuses on 'effectiveness' or 'what works' not only fails to engage with the obvious question of 'effective for what?', but also neglects the valuable questions of how education and educational practice should be understood, of what education is for (Deng, 2024). A related concern is that the policy leads to a lack of focus on issues of curriculum (Poulton & Golledge, 2024). The risk is that algorithmic control of practice ends up frustrating education's purposes – even the narrow ones it is supposed to promote of improved results (Burnett & Coldwell, 2021).

Accountability and compliance pressures also overshadow the relationship between research and practice (Puttick, 2017), and this means we continue to neglect more grounded and meaningful interaction between teachers and research (Hoath & Podesta, 2020) and focus instead on enacting what works with fidelity.

Expecting this kind of enactment of guidance from predictive research draws attention away from understanding the judgements that teachers must make, because teaching is so contingent on context and on the competing aims and purposes of education (Biesta, 2013). It also means that we neglect the role played by teachers' exercise of judgement in developing practical wisdom through experience and problem solving (Biesta, 2007, p. 11), and perhaps even in responding to contemporary crises of recruitment and retention (Procter-Legg et al., 2025; Swift et al., 2024).

EBE has not been allowed to develop a better understanding of ways to evaluate research or the value of different approaches to research. This is because EBE only recognises one form of research inquiry – large-scale RCTs producing statistical evidence of effect size. Arguably, it also recognises only one kind of researcher – the cognitive psychologist (Wrigley & McCusker, 2019). Even very basic distinctions between explanatory research (which looks at whether something might 'work' in ideal conditions) and pragmatic research (which considers if, how and when it works in real conditions of practice) (Mykhalovskiy & Weir, 2004) have not yet been commonly recognised in the policy implementation of EBE. We should recognise and welcome the increasing use of RCT methods in classroom-based trials (Connolly et al., 2018) and the way that the EEF has recently studied the impact of popular 'cognitive science' teaching techniques outside the lab (Perry et al., 2021). However, we should also recognise that the results of these emerging pragmatic studies suggest that many of the 'what works' approaches promoted by influential explanatory research have much smaller effects in real-world situations (Moss & France, 2023; Perry et al., 2021).

How Has EBE Reacted to These Debates?

The response of the EBE movement to the disappointing impact of 'what works' on the ground has unfortunately focused on deficits in implementation. This places any fault at the door of either (1) the researchers, for not using sufficient rigour in choosing interventions to study or which outcome measures to use, or (2) the teachers, for not really being willing to change what they are doing, or failing to understand (and therefore reproduce with 'fidelity') the technique they are supposed to be using (Moss & France, 2023). The idea of 'lethal mutations' has formed a key part of this response (Kirschner & Hendrick, 2024; Perry et al., 2021). This catchy phrase suggests that 'what works' would work if only teachers would learn to do as they are instructed. The phrase does an interesting job of simultaneously downplaying the importance of professional judgement in the 'intelligent adaptation of evidence to meet local context and circumstances' (Collins & Coleman, 2021, p. 25; cited in Moss & France, 2023) whilst also comparing such adaptation to a kind of genetic corruption.

It might instead be more accurate to argue that, in reality, the concept of evidence-based practice has been corrupted and simplified in the transfer from medicine to teaching (McKnight & Morgan, 2020). Policy makers, and some of the researchers and school leaders together promoting EBE have only selected those parts of the idea and experience of EBM that already met their own interests. They have failed to learn from the lessons of 40 years of its development, or to understand the differences between the practice of medicine and that of teaching (McKnight & Morgan, 2023). Moreover, challenge and criticism of EBE have been stifled, through indirect and direct means by targeting university-based teacher educators through a kind of 'discourse of derision' (Ball, 1990) and by narrowing funding for educational research. However, it is worth noting that frustration in the educational research community has also resulted in unhelpful or divisive language (Menzies, 2024). Connolly, for example, points out how the dismissive language about quantitative methods seeks to put that approach 'on trial', and pre-determine the purposes of educational research in ways that exclude the concerns and aims of those who have rightly questioned the role and impact of evidence on teaching practice (Connolly et al., 2018, pp. 277–278).

NEW (AND OLD) IDEAS ABOUT THE RELATIONSHIP BETWEEN RESEARCH AND PRACTICE

Rather than abandon the aim of better use of evidence in educational practice, we need to build bridges between research and practice. We need to make a determined effort to recognise and legitimise the call for a greater role for 'evidence' in practice, and those who challenge the specific ways in which that call is being promoted (Menzies, 2024).

A Broader Definition of Research

A first step might be to broaden our collective understanding of what evidence and research are, and how they interact with education and its stakeholders (Clegg, 2005). Laurence Stenhouse's description of research as 'systematic self-critical inquiry' (Stenhouse, 1981) is a useful way of doing this. A broad range of academic, scholarly and research activity could sit within such a minimal definition, but it does not mean that 'anything goes', because of the way that Stenhouse explains its constituent parts.

'Inquiry' refers to the researcher's curiosity, and their need to understand, but does not place a limit on who or where that researcher is. 'Systematic' requires a sustained focus on the issues, through the carrying out of a plan, but does not limit the kinds of evidence or methods that the plan might require. 'Self-critical' means that researchers have to be open and transparent about their methods, aims and data. It also means be cautious about accepting 'received and comfortable answers' and carefully test the ideas and theories that they themselves brings to the activity.

This inclusive definition of research provides criteria for helping us decide how (and if) to take such research into account in our practice. It also does not exclude those forms of research that policymakers have preferred. In Stenhouse's view, research based on predictive statistical modelling can be helpful in setting 'groundrules' for educational practice and understanding the context in which they are developed and enacted; but they cannot dictate specific practices in real-life contexts (Stenhouse, 1981).

A broader understanding of the value of different types of research and evidence might enrich EBE, in allowing researchers and teachers to understand the value and characteristics of a range of types of research, such as high-quality case studies, of qualitative research which explores the context and purposes of education, and which takes into account the need for practitioners to develop and exercise judgement. There is no reason why these kinds of research cannot also work alongside the kinds of large-scale, quantitative and controlled studies that policy makers also value. This approach might also promote research questions that teachers are really interested in.

CASE STUDY – WHAT WOULD TEACHERS RESEARCH?

An important element of the criticism of Educational Research was that research decisions and topics were decided without reference to the ideas or needs of the profession (Hargreaves, 2007). For instance, Ben Goldacre, a science journalist, who championed the role of RCTs in Educational Research, suggested that we 'identify questions that matter to practitioners' (Cain & Allan, 2017).

In response to this critique, a group of researchers decided to investigate which research questions seemed most important to teachers (Everton et al., 2000). Their participant teachers chose from a list of pre-determined research topics, but were also asked to suggest other topics that interested them. The pre-determined topic most often chosen was the comparison of effectiveness of different strategies (61%), followed by effective classroom teacher behaviour (57%), strategies for different levels of 'ability' (54%), motivation and disengagement (50%), developing creative thinking (45%) and 'effective whole class teaching' (40%). The topics suggested by teachers were varied and often unique, but 143 of the 240 suggestions could be grouped into broad areas:

- 'Curriculum', including issues of progress and wider curriculum purposes.
- 'Learning' – including pupils' relations to school and each other.
- 'Home and school links' – relationships with and working with parents.

Only two issues – working with parents, and pupils' self-esteem and motivation were chosen more than 10 times, suggesting that these were important issues for the profession (Everton et al., 2000).

It is interesting to note that these self-directed questions do not primarily focus on the need for solutions that 'work' irrespective of context – but instead on the variety of challenges implied by teachers' work. This suggests that we are missing out on an important resource for directing educational research with impact – the interests and needs of serving teachers.

Reflective Questions

- What are the main challenges of your practice, where you teach?
- What broader questions about education, society and school interest you?
- What questions do you think might interest your pupils?

A Discipline of Education

If we agree on the need for a broader, more nuanced and more rigorous definition of research and research purposes, the next steps are to consider the relationship between research and practice, and the context in which both take place (Deng, 2024). Instead of simply applying findings from related disciplines, a re-imagined 'educational discipline' could involve learning from and working with experts in other fields, in order to focus on improving teaching as a practical and deliberative activity (Deng, 2024, p. 777). This would promote a kind of 'intelligent action' (Garrison, 1999) in which practitioners can find strategies which reflect their knowledge and insights from research and experience, as well as their values and the shifting priorities that are formed in the act of teaching. This 'discipline' could cover a much broader range of topics than 'what works', including the impact of society and policy on teaching. However, the context of practice – the work of teachers in planning, teaching, marking, liaising, and accounting for their work, would be a key element (Deng, 2024). In this way, a focus, on 'instruction under the conditions of schooling as distinct from other instructional settings' (Gundem, 2000, p. 23, cited in Hudson, 2024) might allow us to find more constructive approaches to the research practice gap, especially as the results of EBE (Perry et al., 2021) and the lessons of EBM (Greenhalgh, 2014a) suggest that ignoring or arguing context away is unlikely to work.

CONCLUSION – OVERCOMING BARRIERS

Several barriers must be overcome if this new and more fruitful relationship between research and education practice is to be realised, but we will consider only three prominent ones before closing. Overcoming these barriers is especially urgent in democracies (Elliott, 2024; Holloway & Larsen Hedegaard, 2023) where we need to rediscover the power of sustained encounter and engagement with diverse perspectives (Biesta, 2020) in shared institutional frameworks (Snyder, 2017).

The first is that research can only be of value to teachers if it is open to evaluation and critique by professionals, politicians and other researchers. This means that policymakers and researchers must learn to address each other's concerns in ways that do not dissolve into name-calling and derision. Policy makers must be prepared to fund research and academic activities which is able to call out 'policy masquerading as research', but researchers must value rigour in research and seek to make our own research and claims rigorously (Day, 1997). Researchers and practitioners must work together to find ways to improve research and communicate findings in ways that are transparently accessible. This book is an attempt to do just that.

This implies, secondly, that we must recognise teachers', pupils' and other stakeholders' agency. This is another neglected lesson of EBM, where the values, purposes and experience of patients have become increasingly important and where the focus on practitioners' judgement and knowledge remains a central pillar of professionalism. Some of the chapters in this book make a contribution to this step in helping teachers use and even undertake research. These chapters also expand our idea of who takes part in research, including a the role for children as researchers.

These two aspects come together in overcoming the final barrier, of recognising a more dialogical relationship between 'evidence' and 'practice'. Following EBM, but going beyond in ways that reflect the characteristics of education, we must allow for research which goes further than looking for 'what works', or even 'what works when or where'. We must be able to ask the kinds of broad questions that Deng's Discipline of Education would facilitate, and be able to consider our collective educational work in the light of those findings.

> **REVIEW OF CHAPTER OBJECTIVES**
>
> Now that you have read this chapter, you should be able to:
>
> - Explain what educational research is and how it relates to teaching, learning, and policy.
> - Understand the development and critique of EBE, especially in comparison to EBM.
> - Identify and reflect on the various ways teachers can use research in their professional practice (instrumental, symbolic, conceptual).
> - Consider the importance of teacher judgement and context in applying research, and explore broader, pragmatic definitions of research in education.

REFERENCES

Arquero, J. L. (2023). The extreme relevance of avoiding the file drawer effect in educational research (editorial). *EDUCADE – Revista de Educación En Contabilidad, Finanzas y Administración de Empresas, 14,* 1–4. https://doi.org/10.12795/EDUCADE.2023.i14.01

Ball, S. J. (1990). *Politics and policy making in education: Explorations in sociology.* Routledge.

Bergeron, P.-J., & Rivard, L. (2017). How to engage in pseudoscience with real data: A criticism of John Hattie's arguments in visible learning from the perspective of a statistician. *McGill Journal of Education/Revue Des Sciences de l'éducation de McGill, 52*(1), 237–246. https://doi.org/10.7202/1040816ar

Biesta, G. (2007). Why "what works" won't work: Evidence-based practice and the democratic deficit in educational research. *Educational Theory, 57*(1), 1–22. https://doi.org/10.1111/j.1741-5446.2006.00241.x

Biesta, G. (2013). Receiving the gift of teaching: From 'learning from' to 'being taught by'. *Studies in Philosophy and Education, 32*(5), 449–461. https://doi.org/10.1007/s11217-012-9312-9

Biesta, G. (2020). What constitutes the good of education? Reflections on the possibility of educational critique. *Educational Philosophy and Theory*, 52(10), 1023–1027. https://doi.org/10.1080/00131857.2020.1723468

Blunkett, D. (2000). *Influence or irrelevance: Can social science improve government?—Secretary of state's ESRC lecture speech 2nd February 2000*. Economic and Social Research Council and Department for Education & Employment.

Blunt, C. (2015). *Hierarchies of evidence in evidence-based medicine* [PhD, London School of Economics and Political Science]. https://etheses.lse.ac.uk/3284/?trk=public_post_comment-text

Burnett, C., & Coldwell, M. (2021). Randomised controlled trials and the interventionisation of education. *Oxford Review of Education*, 47(4), 423–438. https://doi.org/10.1080/03054985.2020.1856060

Cain, T., & Allan, D. (2017). The invisible impact of educational research. *Oxford Review of Education*, 43(6), 718–732. https://doi.org/10.1080/03054985.2017.1316252

Claridge, J. A., & Fabian, T. C. (2005). History and development of evidence-based medicine. *World Journal of Surgery*, 29(5), 547–553. https://doi.org/10.1007/s00268-005-7910-1

Clarke, M., & Ravindran, V. (2019). Royal College of Physicians of Edinburgh, James Lind Library and fair tests of treatment. *Journal of the Royal College of Physicians of Edinburgh*, 49(4), 267–268. https://doi.org/10.4997/jrcpe.2019.401

Clegg, S. (2005). Evidence-based practice in educational research: A critical realist critique of systematic review. *British Journal of Sociology of Education*, 26(3), 415–428. https://doi.org/10.1080/01425690500128932

Coe, R. (2002). It's the effect size, stupid. *British Educational Research Association Annual Conference*, 12, 14. https://f.hubspotusercontent30.net/hubfs/5191137/attachments/ebe/ESguide.pdf

Coe, R., Waring, M., Hedges, L. V., Ashley, L. D., & Robert Coe, M. W. (2021). *Research methods and methodologies in education* (3rd ed., p. i). SAGE Publications Ltd.

Collins, K. (2018a, January 26). *Address to evidence fair*. Blackpool Research School. Evidence Fair January 2018. https://researchschool.org.uk/blackpool/news/evidence-fair-25th-january-2018

Collins, K. (2018b, March 26). *Kevan Collins: Gathering evidence of what techniques work in the classroom should be welcomed* [Blog]. Conservative Home. https://conservativehome.mystagingwebsite.com/2018/03/26/kevan-collins-gathering-evidence-of-what-techniques-work-in-the-classroom-should-be-welcomed/

Collins, K., & Coleman, R. (2021). Evidence-informed policy and practice. In P. Earley & T. Greany (Eds.), *School leadership and education system reform* (p. 19). Bloomsbury.

Connolly, P., Keenan, C., & Urbanska, K. (2018). The trials of evidence-based practice in education: A systematic review of randomised controlled trials in education research 1980–2016. *Educational Research*, *60*(3), 276–291. https://doi.org/10.1080/00131881.2018.1493353

Craske, J. (2021). Logics, rhetoric and 'the blob': Populist logic in the conservative reforms to English schooling. *British Educational Research Journal*, *47*(2), 279–298. https://doi.org/10.1002/berj.3682

Davies, P. (1999). What is evidence-based education? *British Journal of Educational Studies*, *47*(2), 108–121. https://doi.org/10.1111/1467-8527.00106

Day, C. (1997). Being a professional in schools and universities: Limits, purposes and possibilities for development. *British Educational Research Journal*, *32*(1), 193–208.

Deng, Z. (2024). Practice, pedagogy and education as a discipline: Getting beyond close-to-practice research. *British Educational Research Journal*, *50*(2), 772–793. https://doi.org/10.1002/berj.3951

Didau, D. (2014). *What works is a lot better than what doesn't – David Didau [Blog]*. Learning Spy. https://learningspy.co.uk/myths/make-stick-works-better-doesnt-2/

Djulbegovic, B., & Guyatt, G. H. (2017). Progress in evidence-based medicine: A quarter century on. *The Lancet*, *390*(10092), 415–423. https://doi.org/10.1016/S0140-6736(16)31592-6

Durant, J., Evans, G., & Thomas, G. (1992). Public understanding of science in Britain: The role of medicine in the popular representation of science. *Public Understanding of Science*, *1*(2), 161–182. https://doi.org/10.1088/0963-6625/1/2/002

Edovald, T., & Nevill, C. (2021). Working out what works: The Case of the Education Endowment Foundation in England. *ECNU Review of Education*, 4(1), 46–64. https://doi.org/10.1177/2096531120913039

Edwards, D. J. A., Dattilio, F. M., & Bromley, D. B. (2004). Developing evidence-based practice: The role of case-based research. *Professional Psychology: Research and Practice*, 35(6), 589–597. https://doi.org/10.1037/0735-7028.35.6.589

Elliott, J. (2024). The Stenhouse legacy and the development of an applied research in education tradition. *The Curriculum Journal*, 35(4), 706–721. https://doi.org/10.1002/curj.291

Everton, T., Galton, M., & Pell, T. (2000). Teachers' perspectives on educational research: Knowledge and context. *Journal of Education for Teaching*, 26(2), 167–182. https://doi.org/10.1080/02607470050127081

Fernandez, A., Sturmberg, J., Lukersmith, S., Madden, R., Torkfar, G., Colagiuri, R., & Salvador-Carulla, L. (2015). Evidence-based medicine: Is it a bridge too far? *Health Research Policy and Systems*, 13(1), 66. https://doi.org/10.1186/s12961-015-0057-0

Garrison, J. (1999). John Dewey's theory of practical reasoning. *Educational Philosophy and Theory*, 31(3), 291–312. https://doi.org/10.1111/j.1469-5812.1999.tb00467.x

Goldacre, B. (2013, March 18). *Teachers need to drive the research agenda*. The Guardian. http://www.theguardian.com/education/2013/mar/18/teaching-research-michael-gove

Goldenberg, M. J. (2006). On evidence and evidence-based medicine: Lessons from the philosophy of science. *Social Science & Medicine*, 62(11), 2621–2632.

Gorard, S., & Torgerson, C. (2006). *The ESRC researcher development initiative: Promise and pitfalls of pragmatic trials in education*. BERA Annual Conference. https://research.birmingham.ac.uk/en/publications/the-esrc-researcher-development-initiative-promise-and-pitfalls-o

Gove, M. (2013). *Education reform: New national curriculum for schools*. GOV.UK. https://www.gov.uk/government/speeches/education-reform-new-national-curriculum-for-schools

Greenhalgh, T. (2014a). Evidence based medicine: A movement in crisis? *BMJ: British Medical Journal*, *348*, g3725. https://doi.org/10.1136/bmj.g3725

Greenhalgh, T. (2014b). *How to read a paper: The basics of evidence-based medicine* (5th ed.). Wiley-Blackwell.

Gundem, B. B. (2000). Understanding European didactics. In M. Ben-Peretz, A. Sally Brown, & B. Moon (Eds.), *Routledge international companion to education* (pp. 235–262). Routledge.

Hall, D. (2023). England: Neo-liberalism, regulation and populism in the educational reform laboratory. In J. B. Krejsler & L. Moos (Eds.), *School policy reform in Europe: Exploring transnational alignments, national particularities and contestations* (pp. 47–69). Springer.

Hardwicke, T. E., & Wagenmakers, E.-J. (2023). Reducing bias, increasing transparency and calibrating confidence with preregistration. *Nature Human Behaviour*, *7*(1), 15–26. https://doi.org/10.1038/s41562-022-01497-2

Hargreaves, D. H. (1994). The new professionalism: The synthesis of professional and institutional development. *Teaching and Teacher Education*, *10*(4), 423–438. https://doi.org/10.1016/0742-051X(94)90023-X

Hargreaves, D. (2007). Teaching as a research-based profession: Possibilities and prospects (The Teacher Training Agency Lecture 1996). In M. Hammersley (Ed.), *Educational research and evidence-based practice* (pp. 3–17). SAGE Publications.

Hattie, J. (2008). *Visible learning: A synthesis of over 800 meta-analyses relating to achievement* (1st ed.). Routledge.

Hegedus, E. J., & Moody, J. (2010). Clinimetrics corner: The many faces of selection bias. *The Journal of Manual & Manipulative Therapy*, *18*(2), 69–73. https://doi.org/10.1179/106698110X12640740712699

Hoath, L., & Podesta, E. (2020). The context in which teachers exercise agency and autonomy in directing and completing their own research: A teacher-led, academic-facilitated research group. *Practice*, *2*(supp. 1), 73–85. https://doi.org/10.1080/25783858.2020.1834827

Holloway, J., & Larsen Hedegaard, M. L. (2023). Democracy and teachers: The im/possibilities for pluralisation in evidence-based practice. *Journal of Education Policy*, *38*(3), 432–451. https://doi.org/10.1080/02680939.2021.2014571

Hordern, J., & Brooks, C. (2023). The core content framework and the 'new science' of educational research. *Oxford Review of Education*, *49*(6), 800–818. https://doi.org/10.1080/03054985.2023.2182768

Hordern, J., & Brooks, C. (2024). Towards instrumental trainability in England? The 'Official Pedagogy' of the core content framework. *British Journal of Educational Studies*, *72*(1), 5–22. https://doi.org/10.1080/00071005.2023.2255894

Hudson, B. (2024). *Why no subject didactics in England?* University of Sussex. https://sussex.figshare.com/articles/chapter/Why_no_Subject_Didactics_in_England_/25808995

Jones, K. (2023). *The researchED guide to cognitive science: An evidence-informed guide for teachers*. Hachette UK.

Kirschner, P. A., & Hendrick, C. (2024). *How learning happens: Seminal works in educational psychology and what they mean in practice* (2nd ed.). Routledge. https://doi.org/10.4324/9781003395713

Mann, H., & Djulbegovic, B. (2013). Comparator bias: Why comparisons must address genuine uncertainties. *Journal of the Royal Society of Medicine*, *106*(1), 30–33. https://doi.org/10.1177/0141076812474779

Mason-Wilkes, W. (2018). *Science as religion? Science communication and elective modernism* [PhD]. https://orca.cardiff.ac.uk/id/eprint/109735/

McKnight, L., & Morgan, A. (2020). A broken paradigm? What education needs to learn from evidence-based medicine. *Journal of Education Policy*, *35*(5), 648–664. https://doi.org/10.1080/02680939.2019.1578902

McKnight, L., & Morgan, A. (2023). "Good" choices vs "what really works": A comparison of evidence-based practice in medicine and education. *The Australian Educational Researcher*, *50*(3), 643–659. https://doi.org/10.1007/s13384-022-00509-4

Menzies, L. (2024). 'Populism' and competing epistemic communities in English educational policy: A response to Craske and Watson. *British Educational Research Journal*, *50*(3), 1576–1593. https://doi.org/10.1002/berj.3950

Moss, G., & France, R. (2023). Professional knowledge and research-informed practice: Time for a rethink? *Impact: Journal of the Chartered College of Teaching*, *19*, 10. https://discovery.ucl.ac.uk/id/eprint/10185369/

Mykhalovskiy, E., & Weir, L. (2004). The problem of evidence-based medicine: Directions for social science. *Social Science & Medicine*, 59(5), 1059–1069.

Page, M. J., McKenzie, J. E., Kirkham, J., Dwan, K., Kramer, S., Green, S., & Forbes, A. (2014). Bias due to selective inclusion and reporting of outcomes and analyses in systematic reviews of randomised trials of healthcare interventions. *Cochrane Database of Systematic Reviews*, (10), Art. No.: MR000035. https://doi.org/10.1002/14651858.MR000035.pub2

Perry, T., Lea, R., Jørgensen, C. R., Cordingley, P., Shapiro, K., & Youdell, D. (2021). *Cognitive science approaches in the classroom: A review of the evidence*. EEF. https://educationendowmentfoundation.org.uk/public/files/Publications/Cognitive_science_approaches_in_the_classroom_-_A_review_of_the_evidence.pdf

Philpott, C., & Poultney, V. (2025). *Evidence-based teaching: A critical overview for enquiring teachers* (1st ed.). Routledge. https://doi.org/10.4324/9781041055556

Pirrie, A. (2001). Evidence-based practice in education: The best medicine? *British Journal of Educational Studies*, 49(2), 124–136. https://doi.org/10.1111/1467-8527.t01-1-00167

Poulton, P., & Golledge, C. (2024). Future curriculum-makers: The role of professional experience placements as sites of learning about curriculum-making for preservice teachers. *The Curriculum Journal*, 35(4), 652–672. https://doi.org/10.1002/curj.252

Puttick, S. (2017). 'You'll see that everywhere': Institutional isomorphism in secondary school subject departments. *School Leadership & Management*, 37(1–2), 61–79. https://doi.org/10.1080/13632434.2017.1293633

Procter-Legg, T., Snell, R. J. S., & Klassen, R. M. (2025). The five-year itch: Motivational factors that influence the career decisions of early career teachers in England. *British Educational Research Journal*, 00, 1–25. https://doi.org/10.1002/berj.4149

Renedo, A., Komporozos-Athanasiou, A., & Marston, C. (2018). Experience as evidence: The dialogic construction of health professional knowledge through patient involvement. *Sociology*, 52(4), 778–795. https://doi.org/10.1177/0038038516682457

Sackett, D. L., Rosenberg, W. M. C., Gray, J. A. M., Haynes, R. B., & Richardson, W. S. (1996). Evidence based medicine: What it is and what it isn't. *BMJ*, *312*(7023), 71–72. https://doi.org/10.1136/bmj.312.7023.71

Severs, J. (2022). Nick Gibb: 'We had to blow up the concrete'. *Tes Magazine*. https://www.tes.com/magazine/analysis/general/nick-gibb-interview-we-had-to-blow-up-concrete

Slavin, R. E. (2002). Evidence-based education policies: Transforming educational practice and research. *Educational Researcher*, *31*(7), 15–21. https://doi.org/10.3102/0013189X031007015

Snyder, T. (2017). *On tyranny: Twenty lessons from the twentieth century* (1st ed.). Bodley Head.

Stenhouse, L. (1981). What counts as research? *British Journal of Educational Studies*, *29*(2), 103–114.

Sullivan, G. M. (2011). Getting off the "gold standard": Randomized controlled trials and education research. *Journal of Graduate Medical Education*, *3*(3), 285–289. https://doi.org/10.4300/JGME-D-11-00147.1

Sur, R. L., & Dahm, P. (2011). History of evidence-based medicine. *Indian Journal of Urology*, *27*(4), 487. https://doi.org/10.4103/0970-1591.91438

Swift, D., Clowes, G., Gilbert, S., & Lambert, A. (2024). Sustaining professionalism: Teachers as co-enquirers in curriculum design. *The Curriculum Journal*, *35*(4), 622–636. https://doi.org/10.1002/curj.267

van der Bles, A. M., van der Linden, S., Freeman, A. L. J., Mitchell, J., Galvao, A. B., Zaval, L., & Spiegelhalter, D. J. (2019). Communicating uncertainty about facts, numbers and science. *Royal Society Open Science*, *6*(5), 181870. https://doi.org/10.1098/rsos.181870

Wiliam, D. (2019). Some reflections on the role of evidence in improving education. *Educational Research and Evaluation*, *25*(1–2), 127–139. https://doi.org/10.1080/13803611.2019.1617993

Wrigley, T., & McCusker, S. (2019). Evidence-based teaching: A simple view of "science". *Educational Research and Evaluation*, *25*(1–2), 110–126. https://doi.org/10.1080/13803611.2019.1617992

9

BECOMING AND BEING A CRITICAL TEACHER-RESEARCHER

Amanda Nuttall

Leeds Trinity University, UK

CHAPTER OBJECTIVES

In this chapter, you will:

- Explore conceptualisations of the way teachers work with research.
- Review models of teacher research.
- Reflect on teacher research from critical and humanistic perspectives.
- Begin to understand how teaching and researching can influence identity[ies].

Keywords: Teacher research; practitioner inquiry; action research; teacher identity; critical research

INTRODUCTION

The commitment to establish and support teachers' research activity has a long history in the UK as well as internationally. Much of our current understanding of teacher research activity is founded in work from the 1970s and 1980s, a time when there was a significant movement to share teacher research around curriculum and pedagogical development. One key voice was Lawrence Stenhouse, a history teacher at the time, who endorsed the value of teachers' research activities and offered an enduring definition of such work as 'systematic inquiry made public' (Stenhouse, 1980, p. 1).

In the years that have followed, teachers' relationships *with* research and *as* researchers have been frequently debated and contested. In this chapter, we consider current models of teacher research and some influences on the place and space for research in initial and continuing teacher education. A case study is shared to prompt reflection on what it means to be a critical teacher-researcher, examining the impact that becoming a teacher-researcher can have on an individual's identity[ies]. In conclusion, the transformational potential of critical and intellectual research work for the teaching profession is highlighted.

TEACHERS AND RESEARCH

A large-scale report into the state and future of educational research by the Royal Society and the British Academy in 2018 described a complex ecosystem of educational research within and across the four jurisdictions of the UK. This ecosystem involves a multitude of sites and actors, but the report raised concerns about how teachers in England are positioned as 'consumers' of large-scale, external research knowledge (The Royal Society & The British Academy, 2018). This notion of 'consumerism' is integral in much work around teacher education and professional learning, with concerns raised that teachers in England tend to be situated as passive recipients of new ideas created by 'others', an approach that has been shown to rarely lead to any long-term or meaningful change of professional practices (Keay et al., 2019). Indeed, Hordern and Brooks (2023) argue that current frameworks in initial and continuing teacher education actively undermine teacher professionalism and teacher expertise by leaving little, if any, room for teachers' scholarly and critical research work. These concerns are not a recent phenomenon: nearly 50 years ago Lawrence Stenhouse argued that teachers should be both users *and* subjects of educational research, generating their own research findings on teaching and learning which would invigorate pedagogy in their own classrooms and beyond (Stenhouse, 1980).

But teachers working actively *as* researchers can be problematic. Wyse et al. (2018), in their report on 'Close-to-Practice Research', raise concerns about perceptions of the quality and worth of 'academic' research and 'practice-based' or 'classroom' research. Implicit (and at times explicit) in this these concerns are value judgements, which see academic research as reliable, valid, generalisable and a reputable source of new knowledge, and classroom or practice-based research as localised, context-laden and having little impact beyond the immediate professional space in which it takes place (Hogan & Malone, 2023). While this report offers substantial recommendations for increasing teachers' research activity, it appears that a great deal of this work is considered to be of low or modest quality in comparison to the work of academics or large-scale research bodies. For example, the work of the Education Endowment Foundation[1] (EEF) is prioritised by policymakers, including Department for Education (DfE) and Ofsted, in England. The EEF aims to facilitate large-scale and systematic research use in schools by promoting accessible syntheses of research findings in ways that can be directly applied to school practice and policy.

While much of the work of the EEF may be rigorous and well-meant (including a focus on improving outcomes for the most disadvantaged), there is an explicit research paradigm at play which prioritises scientific approaches to finding and promoting 'what works'. Such a paradigm may be useful in producing syntheses of particular research studies, but these tend to be predicated on a narrow view of the purpose of education, tied to outcomes in standardised testing at all levels of schooling and neglecting to demonstrate concern for the development of pupils or teachers as critical, intellectual individuals (Hordern, 2021; Hordern & Brooks, 2023). Furthermore, the research base of the initial teacher training and early career framework (ITTECF), much of which is drawn from the EEF and similar organisations, such as the Sutton Trust, is claimed to be 'the best available educational research' (Department for Education, 2019, p. 10). As such, compliance and fidelity with this externally mandated body of 'legitimate' research is enforced by DfE and Ofsted (Ellis, 2024). It is not surprising, then, that many teachers continue to ascribe to the 'theory-practice divide', where research belongs in university ivory towers and is seen as irrelevant to their day-to-day classroom practice (Thomson & Riddle, 2018).

However, it has been suggested that teachers' engagement in their own research activity can encourage action and reflection which serves a variety of interests and purposes, from tackling classroom based practice problems to engaging with wider social movements and shining a light on existing inequalities for some children (Daly et al., 2020). But teacher research at any level can be problematic given a policy and practice environment in England which prioritises 'silver bullets' (Lewis & Hogan, 2019) and a 'what works' agenda (Biesta, 2017). As a result, teachers can be positioned as passive in relation to research: as merely receivers and implementers of evidence-informed practices from select research bodies, such as the EEF. Further issues are raised around centrally selected and mandated evidence bases which tend to sustain and reproduce narrow measures of educational quality, school effectiveness and school improvement (Wrigley, 2018). In such an environment answers are privileged over questions and teachers' research activity seems actively discouraged (Beckett & Nuttall, 2019).

REFLECTIVE QUESTIONS

- How do you draw on research to inform your professional reflection?
- What challenges do you have in accessing and working with research?

- How do you currently integrate research into your classroom practice, and what impact does this have?
- How might you collaborate with others to support your research activity and professional development?

PRACTITIONER INQUIRY AND ACTION RESEARCH

Practitioner inquiry, often closely related to notions of action research, is a systematic and reflective process by which teachers investigate their own practices to improve both their teaching and pupil outcomes. In England, this approach is often underpinned by encouraging deeply reflective practices throughout initial teacher training and early career teacher activities and mentoring. As highlighted elsewhere in this book, Clarke and Hollingsworth (2002) depict a complex model of teachers' professional learning and growth in which multiple interconnecting domains are at play. Linking to their model, we can see that teachers who seek to participate in inquiry or action research have the opportunity to develop a critical perspective on their practice, identifying specific issues within their classrooms or schools and responding to these. Through iterative cycles of planning, acting, observing, and reflecting, teachers engage in a continuous quest for improvement, ultimately leading to more effective pedagogies and better educational experiences for their pupils. Such activity, where teachers become leaders of their own research activity, is a considerable step-change to the notion of teachers as compliant and passive consumers of others' research. What is brought to attention here is the way in which teachers' knowledge, practices, values and beliefs can be informed and shaped by their engagement in their own research, alongside the research findings of others, but that this is a complex process rather than a simple application of 'what works' in order to achieve an expected outcome (Biesta & Aldridge, 2021). See Chapters 4 and 5 for further information.

Two influential authors in the field of practitioner inquiry and action research, both of whom draw out complexity in their work, are John Elliott and Susan Groundwater-Smith. John Elliott, a prominent figure in educational research and action research, has emphasised the importance of reflective practice as a means for teachers to transform their understanding of teaching and learning (Elliott, 1993, 2015). His work underlines the idea that through inquiry, teachers can develop a deeper awareness of the complexities of their classroom environments, thereby enhancing their pedagogical skills and pupil outcomes. Similarly, Susan Groundwater-Smith and colleagues have contributed significantly to the discourse around practitioner inquiry, advocating for collaborative action research as a way to harness expertise within and across the teaching community (Groundwater-Smith, 2019; Groundwater-Smith & Mockler, 2009). Groundwater-Smith enhances the work of Elliott, building the participatory aspects of inquiry, which encourages teachers to work together, affording diverse perspectives and shared accountability in addressing educational challenges. Taken together, ideas about the transformative potential of practitioner inquiry and action research foster not only individual teacher improvement but also underpin actions taken to influence systemic changes within the education system.

WHAT MAKES TEACHER RESEARCH *CRITICAL*?

The concerns that have been raised about teachers' research activity in the English context focus on the dominance of cause-and-effect logic, where answers are privileged over questions. Yet there is an established school of thought that the most meaningful and critical forms of teacher research activity are highly complex but can lead to enlightenment and rich cultural understandings. Here, it is useful to consider Carr and Kemmis' (1986) critical framework, which outlines three differentiated levels of teacher research activity. The first level is 'technical', where concern lies with the effective attainment of given goals, for example, meeting a predefined set of professional standards. A list of consensual criteria is specified and linked to short-term goals: these criteria often correspond to broadly defined 'efficacy' criteria, such as results of standardised tests or progress measures, which are teachers' priority concerns (McIntyre, 1993).

The second level is 'practical', where teachers concentrate on evaluating and developing their own teaching. The focus here lies in teachers' articulation and justification of how effective they perceive their practice to be. Moving beyond the technical level, teachers develop their own criteria and use sources of evidence to support decisions and conclusions (Sachs, 2016). However, it is the third, 'critical or emancipatory' level, which holds the potential to be most transformative for teachers. At this level, teachers' concerns move to encompass wider social contexts and movements, including policy, politics and societal forces. They may come to consider conflict between dominant policies and practices and perceived moral and ethical responsibilities as a teacher. This speaks to issues of social justice as teacher research at this level is located in a sociological paradigm where systems come under scrutiny and outcomes of research deliberately challenge the status quo (Nuttall & Beckett, 2020). To reach this level of research requires teachers to be proficient in critical reflexivity, where they are aware of and able to challenge inherent values of education as related to their current and future practice[s] (Hogan & Malone, 2023). However, this can be challenging for teachers as,

> *When practitioner researchers work from an inquiry stance, they are working both within and against the system – an ongoing process, from the inside, of problematizing fundamental assumptions about the purposes of the existing education system and raising difficult questions about educational resources, processes and outcomes. Cochran-Smith and Lytle (2009, p. 146)*

REFLECTIVE QUESTIONS

- **Professional practice:** Can you identify specific areas in your teaching that could benefit from further inquiry?

- **Impact on pupil outcomes:** How might your inquiry help to develop pupil outcomes or their experiences in your classroom?

- **Collaboration**: How might you collaborate with colleagues to develop a community of inquiry?
- **Navigating complexity**: What potential challenges do you see in transitioning from a technical or practical level of teacher research to a critical or emancipatory level?
- **Social justice**: What are the most important broader social, political or ethical issues that affect your work at the moment?

TEACHER AND RESEARCHER IDENTITY[IES]

Teacher research is not just a technical exercise. As Cohen et al. (2011, p. 3) point out, 'research is concerned with understanding the world and that is informed by how we view our world(s), what we take understanding to be, and what we see as the purposes of understanding'. In other words, the ways in which teachers engage with research goes to the very core of their values, beliefs and indeed identity[ies] as a teacher. Teacher identity[ies] itself is a complex domain. The various constructions and definitions of teacher identity in research literature tend to share a common view that an individual's identity is neither a singular nor a fixed attribute of that person and that there are significant relational aspects in identity [re]formation. These aspects include, but are not limited to, notions of identity as: occupying multiple roles and belonging to multiple groups; continuous and self-fashioning; and a combination of personal worlds in interaction with cultural forms and social relationships (Holland et al., 1998; Horn et al., 2008). Sachs (2005) asserts that understanding teachers' professional identity[ies] is important because,

> *Teacher professional identity ... stands at the core of the teaching profession. It provides a framework for teachers to construct their own ideas of 'how to be', 'how to act' and 'how to understand their work and their place in society'. Importantly, teacher identity is not something*

> *that is fixed nor is it imposed; rather it is negotiated through experience and the sense that is made of that experience. (p. 15)*

Here, Sachs aligns with a definition of teacher identity[ies] as not fixed or singular. As you read in Chapter 2, teachers should be considered as individuals whose lives and work are influenced and made meaningful by social and cultural experiences as they experience a process of 'becoming' a teacher (Lambert, 2019). The journey of becoming a teacher and forming professional identity[ies] is unique for each individual, but not created in isolation from others (Gibbs, 2006). However, when we consider teachers' identity[ies] as teachers AND as researchers, it is clear that tensions may arise. Perceptions of teachers seem to have shifted away from teaching as a moral, ethical and intellectual endeavour, towards teaching as corporate and marketise, with an emphasis on delivering a narrow curriculum and measurable data outcomes in national standardised testing (Cochran-Smith, 2021). It seems unlikely that many teachers would have a well-established identity as a researcher, as their experiences of teacher education and their early careers would mitigate against this. Therefore, for an individual to achieve a sense of being a critical teacher-researcher would require some reformation of their professional identity[ies].

REFORMING IDENTITY[IES]: A TEACHER-RESEARCHER CONCEPTUAL FRAMEWORK

As we have seen, an individual's identity can be considered in the way that they perceive themselves as occupying multiple roles and belonging to multiple groups (Holland et al., 1998). For the purpose of this chapter, it is useful to think about two particular roles that an individual occupies, teacher and researcher, while also being mindful that these are just two components of an individual's complete identity. We also know that an identity[ies] forms and reforms over time. Therefore, we can gain insights into an individual's identity[ies] if we seek to uncover past, present and future events (Ricœur, 1980).

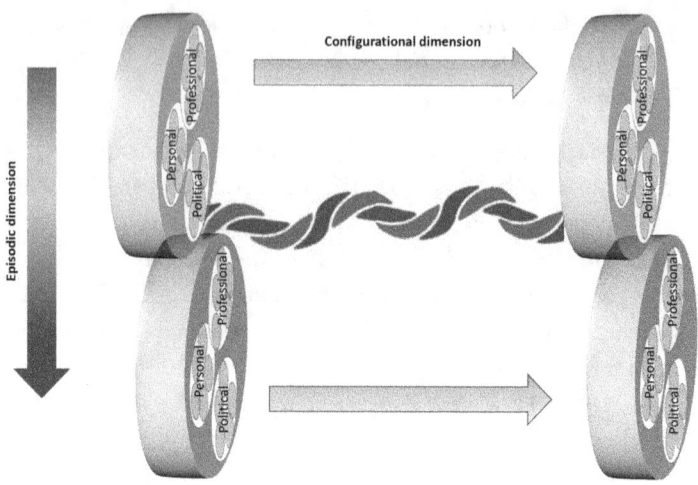

Fig. 9.1. A Rope Metaphor to Explore Teacher-Research Identity[ies].

The framework below uses the metaphor of a rope to bring these ideas together. Interrogating how an individual perceives their teacher and research identity[ies] at one particular moment in time – an episode – helps us to understand if and how these two roles are drawn together in one unified identity. Bringing together multiple episodes over time – the configurational dimension – enables us to draw conclusions about changes over time.

The framework here represents teacher identity[ies] as blue and research identity[ies] as red. That is not to say that these are the only two 'strands' of an individual's identity[ies], but it is a useful framework to help us interrogate teachers' lived experiences in relation to the self as teacher and researcher. The framework also draws upon three discrete 'yarns' of the individual's teacher and researcher strands of identity[ies], acknowledging the complexity and interrelatedness of multiple dimensions.

Personal elements comprise values, beliefs and morals and underpin an individual's motivations for entering and sustaining a career in the teaching profession and for engaging with or sustaining critical research activity. These dimensions may manifest in an individual's emotive responses and reactions to their lived experiences.

Professional elements are negotiated through an individual's interactions with others, including experiences of teacher education and professional learning, and their positioning within a school culture. Social and cultural discourses, including those in popular and social media, can also be significant in shaping aspects of professional dimensions.

Political elements could be understood as the ways in which teachers relate their actions to wider social movements and democratic ideals, along with their perceived sense of agency and autonomy in enacting (or not) policies in their individual classrooms and beyond.

As seen in Fig. 9.1, we can interrogate the inter-relationship between these three elements to shape our understanding of how an individual might form and reform their identity[ies] as a critical teacher-researcher.

CASE STUDY: JANE'S STORY

Jane has been a primary teacher for six years, but has not had a lifelong career in teaching. She had previously owned her own highly successful business, but after selling this, she went to help out at her son's primary school. Not only did she really enjoy the experience, but she also had encouragement from the class teacher to enter the profession. Jane went on to complete an access to education programme, and then a four-year primary education degree programme with a Qualified Teacher Status (QTS) qualification. She then completed a part-time Master's in Education programme and shared her experiences during and after completing her dissertation research project. As reported elsewhere (Nuttall, 2023, 2024), a full exploration of Jane's experiences and her emerging identity as a researcher shows significant transition from 'being interested' in research but seeing it as very separate activity to her daily work as a teacher, to identifying herself as having research 'ingrained' in her personal and professional identity[ies]. For this case study, we can learn through Jane's personal, professional and political experiences some of what it takes to become and be a critical teacher-researcher.

PERSONAL EXPERIENCES

> I was somebody who left school (through illness) with not many qualifications, so I never thought I had the intelligence, or the stamina, to complete a Master's degree… It's been quite a big thing, quite a big achievement. My confidence grew. My passion grew. I've been so personally invested in my research and I've given it my all.

At the start of her dissertation project, Jane described how she didn't feel very confident with research. Part of the challenge was how she saw research as not for 'someone like me'. There are significant links here to influences of gender and social class, as Jane explains how becoming a teacher and then completing her master's was a 'break' away from her past: her family, her community and the peers that she grew up with.

Many in the teaching profession may find that they relate to Jane and her experiences might especially resonate for women and working-class teachers. Although gender and class histories are often unspoken and unexposed (Friedman, 2016) in the teaching profession, these are two highly influential dimensions of personal identity[ies] as a teacher and researcher. Women tend to be over-represented in the teaching profession, especially in early years and primary provision, and in England, 76% of the teaching workforce as a whole is female.[2] Furthermore, teaching, along with other social professions such as nursing and policing, can be an accessible career option for working-class students. But both gender and class identity[ies] can present barriers for teachers who seek to become critical researchers. As Jane said at the start of her research journey, 'I tend to think of researchers as professors, like Robin Alexander, or people who do big projects or who work for the EEF and Sutton Trust'. But Jane came to see herself as a researcher, showing that we should, and can, challenge our personal perceptions so that we can expand possibilities for our own critical, research, and professional learning.

PROFESSIONAL EXPERIENCES

> I am more of an evidence-based, research-based practitioner now. And I see the importance of it! My research has helped me develop so obviously I want to pass that on to help other people to develop their practice.... but changing those mindsets... I'm coming across so much resistance and that has been... interesting.

Jane's experiences, challenges and successes during her research project proved powerful in leading her to [re]consider the role, purpose and value of research across the teaching profession more broadly. But a difficulty that Jane faced during her research project was that she experienced resistance and sometimes apathy towards her work from colleagues. This is not entirely surprising, given the research context described earlier in this chapter, where teachers in England are often expected to 'consume' and apply legitimised evidence and research in very narrow and controlled ways, rather than seeing themselves as active, critical researchers in their own right.

Despite this, Jane continued to advocate for research-informed practice in her school. Over 12 months after finishing her dissertation research project, she described how she was still researching and was encouraging 2 teachers that she now mentored to engage with action research and practitioner inquiry activities in their own classes. And we can learn from Jane's optimism, as she explains, 'I know definitely I've impacted two people in school, which doesn't sound a lot, but if those two then go and influence two other people, then it grows, doesn't it? And it gets it goes out there'. Becoming a critical teacher-researcher starts with a change in ourselves, but also has transformative potential for our colleagues and peers too.

POLITICAL EXPERIENCES

> There seems to be, the same with anything in education, there seems to be these buzzwords and at the moment the buzzword is recovery curriculum.

Jane very rarely mentioned politics related to education or her own lived experience, but she did express a lot of frustration around language and fads in education policy-making. She evoked a sense that buzzwords grab headlines, but she also found that in reality, this is often rhetoric, with no funding, no resources and no real commitment made to effecting any kind of meaningful change. At the heart of this lies implicit criticism of those who have power and agency over policy-making but who are often removed from the day-to-day realities of working with and for children, families, and communities.

As explored in conceptions of teacher research earlier in this chapter, one key driver of practitioner inquiry and action research is social justice which often involves reflexivity and asking critical questions about *why* we engage in particular practices in education and the impact these practices might have on particular groups and individuals (Nuttall & Beckett, 2020). Jane describes feeling disappointed in policies and practices that focus solely on children's progress in reading, writing, and maths, and neglect to show care for the development of the whole child or to connect with children's lives outside of the classroom. These kinds of experiences can make being a critical teacher-researcher uncomfortable as we find ourselves working simultaneously within and against the education system (Mockler & Groundwater-Smith, 2015). However, as Jane shows us, we can use this discomfort to prompt meaningful action in our own classrooms and beyond.

REFLECTIVE QUESTIONS

These questions will help you to take the first steps in analysing a case study. Start by thinking about Jane's story and what she learned about herself as a teacher and a researcher through her lived experiences. Use the prompts to reflect on your own experiences and how you might take forward some of your learning from this chapter.

Personal dimensions: How do you perceive your own identity as a researcher in education? What barriers, if any, do you feel prevent me from fully embracing this identity, similar to Jane's initial feelings? In what ways do your gender, social class, and upbringing influence your experiences and beliefs about teaching and research? How can you acknowledge and navigate these influences in my professional journey?

Professional dimensions: How do you currently integrate research into your teaching practice? In what ways are you able to work with colleagues in engaging with practitioner inquiry and action research? What actions can you take to foster a culture of critical research?

Political dimensions: How do you feel about the current educational policies affecting your practice? Do you see yourself as an agent of change within this system, and if so, how can you align with social justice? How could you use discomfort to provoke action or to advocate for change?

CONCLUSION

When teachers actively engage in research and knowledge building work, critical intellectual conversations about wider issues of education, dominant policy discourses and narratives, and critical theorising of the political context of teachers' work can take place. Such theorising may mean that teachers seek to influence agendas beyond improvement of pupil attainment in their individual schools and go on to challenge the status quo related not just to professional dynamics, but to wider social, cultural, moral, and ethical dimensions. However, this may be challenging, considering that these teachers may find themselves working simultaneously within and against the system (Mockler & Groundwater-Smith, 2015).

The contested and complex nature of research in teaching and teacher education has resulted in teachers' diverse understandings *of* and engagement *with* research-informed learning and professional practice. But to achieve an authentically inquiry-based or research-informed teaching profession, there needs to be a shift from simplistic theory-to-practice dialogues to a rich culture of professional knowledge creation. The case study shared in this chapter highlights how teachers' engagement in critical, intellectual research activity through master's level learning has the potential to provide critical scholarship that underpins systematic inquiry and the creation of new knowledge and understandings, which has the potential to be of benefit outside an individual teacher's immediate classroom context. Such forms of critical scholarship and knowledge work can extend teachers' imagination by opening up alternative policy discourses and narratives which may have been previously hidden. As we saw in Jane's story, these experiences can also significantly influence teachers' own understandings of their personal, professional, and political selves.

Despite this transformative potential, for us in England, dominant narratives and perceptions of teachers portray them as leaving initial teacher training (ITT) as a 'finished product', rather than as lifelong professional learners (e.g., Keay et al., 2019; Nuttall, 2024). How, then, might we take this kind of work forward? Let's return to Stenhouse (1981), who famously claimed that 'It is teachers who in the end will change the world of the school by understanding it'. Here is a call to all of us in education to network, collaborate, and construct spaces where teachers are enabled and encouraged to act systematically as critical researchers and knowledge creators. Transformational potential for individual teachers, and collectively for the profession, can then become a real possibility.

> **REVIEW OF CHAPTER OBJECTIVES**
>
> In this chapter, we have:
>
> - Explored conceptualisations of the way teachers work with research.
> - Critiqued models of teacher research.
> - Reflected on teacher research from critical and humanistic perspectives.
> - Begun to understand how teaching and researching can influence identity[ies].

NOTES

1. The Education Endowment Foundation (EEF) is a large scale, independent charity which seeks to support educational settings to use evidence to improve teaching and learning outcomes. The most common tool used by schools in England is the Teaching and Learning Toolkit, a meta-analysis of educational evidence which ranks potential interventions based on financial costs, strength of evidence and impact on pupil progress, measured in additional months of learning. See *Teaching and Learning Toolkit*, EEF.

2. DfE School Workforce Census (2023/2024). Available at: School workforce in England, Reporting year 2023 – Explore education statistics – GOV.UK.

FURTHER READING

Tatto, M. T., & Menter, I. (Eds.). *Knowledge, policy and practice in learning to teach: A cross-national study*. Bloomsbury.

Wyse, D., Brown, C., Oliver, S., & Poblete, X. (2018). *The BERA close-to-practice research project: Research report*. https://www.bera.ac.uk/project/close-to-practice-research-project

REFERENCES

Beckett, L., & Nuttall, A. (2019). Education and activism. In *Oxford research encyclopedia of education*. Oxford University Press. https://doi.org/10.1093/acrefore/9780190264093.013.375

Biesta, G. (2017). Education, measurement and the professions: Reclaiming a space for democratic professionality in education. *Educational Philosophy and Theory*, 49(4), 315–330.

Biesta, G., & Aldridge, D. (2021). The contested relationships between educational research, theory and practice: Introduction to a special section. *British Educational Research Journal*, 47(6), 1447–1450. https://doi.org/10.1002/berj.3772

Carr, W., & Kemmis, S. (1986). *Becoming critical: Education knowledge and action research*. Falmer.

Clarke, D., & Hollingsworth, H. (2002). Elaborating a model of teacher development. *Teaching and Teacher Education*, *18*(2002), 947–967.

Cochran-Smith, M. (2021). Exploring teacher quality: International perspectives. *European Journal of Teacher Education*, *44*(3), 415–428. https://doi.org/10.1080/02619768.2021.1915276

Cohen, L., Manion, L., & Morrison, K. (2011). *Research methods in education* (7th ed.). Routledge.

Daly, C., Davidge-Smith, L., Williams, C., & Jones, C. (2020). Is there hope for action research in a 'directed profession'? *London Review of Education*, *18*(3), 339–355. https://doi.org/10.14324/LRE.18.3.02

Department for Education. (2019). *Initial teacher training (ITT): Core content framework*. https://www.gov.uk/government/publications/initial-teacher-training-itt-core-content-framework#:~:text=Theinitial teacher training (ITT,anddeliveringtheirITTprogrammes

Elliott, J. (1993). What have we learned from action research in school-based evaluation? *Educational Action Research*, *1*(1), 175–186.

Elliott, J. (2015). Educational action research as the quest for virtue in teaching. *Educational Action Research*, *23*(1), 4–21.

Ellis, V. (2024). *Teacher education in crisis. The state, the market and universities in England*. Bloomsbury Academic.

Friedman, S. (2016). Habitus Clivé and the emotional imprint of social mobility. *Sociological Review*, *64*(1), 129–147. https://doi.org/10.1111/1467-954X.12280

Gibbs, C. (2006). *To be a Teacher: Journeys Towards Authenticity*. Pearson Education.

Groundwater-Smith, S. (2019). *Inquiry-based learning and its enhancement of the practice of teaching*. Oxford Research Encyclopedia of Education. https://oxfordre.com/education/view/10.1093/acrefore/9780190264093.001.0001/acrefore-9780190264093-e-777

Groundwater-Smith, S., & Mockler, N. (2009). *Teacher professional learning in an age of compliance: Mind the gap*. Springer.

Hogan, P., & Malone, A. (2023). Tackling a lingering infirmity: On the nature and warrant of action research in education. *British Educational Research Journal*, *49*(3), 439–454. https://doi.org/10.1002/berj.3849

Holland, D. C., Lachiotte, W., Skinner, D., & Cain, C. (1998). *Identity and agency in cultural worlds*. Harvard University Press.

Hordern, J. (2021). Why close to practice is not enough: Neglecting practice in educational research. *British Educational Research Journal*, *47*(6), 1451–1465. https://doi.org/10.1002/berj.3622

Hordern, J., & Brooks, C. (2023). The core content framework and the 'new science' of educational research. *Oxford Review of Education*, *49*(6), 1–19. https://doi.org/10.1080/03054985.2023.2182768

Horn, I. S., Nolen, S. B., Ward, C. J., & Campbell, S. S. (2008). Developing practices in multiple worlds: The role of identity in learning to teach. *Teacher Education Quarterly*, *35*(3), 61–72.

Keay, J. K., Carse, N., & Jess, M. (2019). Understanding teachers as complex professional learners. *Professional Development in Education*, *45*(1), 125–137.

Lambert, L. (2019). Becoming teacher, becoming researcher: Reconsidering data analysis in post-qualitative practitioner research. *Practice*, *1*(2), 151–168. https://doi.org/10.1080/25783858.2019.1659633

Lewis, S., & Hogan, A. (2019). Reform first and ask questions later? The implications of (fast) schooling policy and 'silver bullet' solutions. *Critical Studies in Education*, *60*(1), 1–18. https://doi.org/10.1080/17508487.2016.1219961

McIntyre, D. (1993). Theory, theorizing and reflection in initial teacher education. In J. Calderhead & P. Gates (Eds.), *Conceptualising reflection in teacher development* (pp. 39–52). Routledge.

Mockler, N., & Groundwater-Smith, S. (2015). Seeking for the unwelcome truths: Beyond celebration in inquiry-based teacher professional learning. *Teachers and Teaching: Theory and Practice*, *21*(5), 603–614.

Nuttall, A. (2023). 'Becoming something bigger and better than you were'. One teacher's experience of identity transition[s] during master's level research. In V. Chiou, L. Geunis, O. Holz, N. Oruç Ertürk, J. Ratkowska-Pasikowska, & F. Shelton (Eds.), *Contemporary challenges in education.*

Paradoxes and illuminations: Voices from the classroom (Vol. 3, pp. 332–346). Waxmann Verlag.

Nuttall, A. (2024). Teachers' experiences of transformational professional learning through Master's level study: Becoming, being and belonging as a teacher and researcher. *British Journal of Educational Studies*, 72(5), 627–644. https://doi.org/10.1080/00071005.2024.2376140

Nuttall, A., & Beckett, L. (2020). Teachers' professional knowledge work on poverty and disadvantage. In L. Beckett (Ed.), *Research-informed teacher learning: Critical perspectives on theory, research and Practice* (pp. 117–131). Routledge.

Ricœur, P. (1980). Narrative time. *Critical Inquiry*, 7(1), 169–190.

Sachs, J. (2005). Teacher education and the development of professional identity: Learning to be a teacher. In P. Denicolo & M. Kompf (Eds.), *Connecting policy and practice: Challenges for teaching and learning in schools and universities* (pp. 5–21). Routledge.

Sachs, J. (2016). Teacher professionalism: Why are we still talking about it? *Teachers and Teaching: Theory and Practice*, 22(4), 413–425.

Stenhouse, L. (1980). The study of samples and the study of cases. *British Educational Research Journal*, 6(1), 1–7.

Stenhouse, L. (1981). What counts as research? *British Journal of Educational Studies*, 29(2), 103–114.

The Royal Society & The British Academy. (2018). *Harnessing educational research*. https://www.bera.ac.uk/wp-content/uploads/2013/12/BERA-RSA-Research-Teaching-Profession-FULL-REPORT-for-web.pdf?noredirect=1

Thomson, P., & Riddle, S. (2018). Who speaks for teachers? Social media and teacher voice. In A. Baroutsis, S. Riddle, & P. Thomson (Eds.), *Education research and the media* (pp. 99–118). Routledge. https://doi.org/10.4324/9781351129114-7

Wrigley, T. (2018). The power of evidence: Reliable science or a set of blunt tools? *British Educational Research Journal*, 44(3), 359–376.

Wyse, D., Brown, C., Oliver, S., & Poblete, X. (2018). *The BERA close-to-practice research project: Research report*. https://www.bera.ac.uk/project/close-to-practice-research-project

CONCLUSION

Megan Stephenson[a], Angela Gill[b] and Ed Podesta[a]

[a]Leeds Trinity University, UK
[b]Durham University, UK

We started this book by stating our intention to challenge the narrow relationship between research and practice in teacher education and professional development, which has dominated policy and practice in recent years. We hope that a book written by authors with diverse teaching and research backgrounds offers multiple perspectives on how research can more meaningfully inform educational practice.

We are confident that this diversity is reflected in the range of issues our authors have focused on, from novice teacher identity and professional dilemmas to ethical research, sustainability, and pupil participation in research. We are arguing for a deeper, more critical, and ethical orientation to educational inquiry. Our challenge to simplistic 'cause and effect' models of evidence used in policy is to show that richer, practice-sensitive approaches can better support adaptive teaching and curriculum innovation, while reinforcing teachers' autonomy and critical engagement.

A recurring theme is the call for more nuanced, 'intelligent' action rather than prescriptive adherence to top-down evidence. We have argued that genuine professional development arises not from technical compliance but from intellectual and ethical engagement with practice. In reasserting the value of research-informed practice as a collaborative, thoughtful, and empowering process for teachers and teacher educators alike, we hope we have underlined a need for a new relationship between research and practice.

However, we also want to make that new relationship more accessible and realisable. Our aim, therefore, was to develop a book that offered practical guidance as well as challenge. One of the important lessons of evidence-based medicine is the importance of creating research and guidance that respects the contexts of practice, empowers practitioners in understanding the purposes and value of the research that confronts them, and that also admits both their concerns and their participation in research. Some chapters, therefore, provide practical strategies, such as toolkits and frameworks for engaging with research. We see value in engagement focused on understanding the processes of research evidence and analysis, but also in practitioners taking part in systematic enquiries, in research that directly addresses their concerns, in their contexts. The frameworks offered here are progressive in that we want to remove barriers to teachers' participation and not put a ceiling on the level of their engagement.

We do recognise the challenges that this approach brings, for policy, practice and research. For policy makers the challenge is for an expansion in the conception of research. This expansion includes a broader understanding of the nature of research, and the nature of the different contributions that research can bring to the practice of education. We are aware that this challenge is a very difficult one in a time of restricted resourcing. If education is to develop a coherent research discipline this needs partly to be achieved through a policy-sponsored development of a research-active HE sector in education. This research should take place in partnership with school teachers and leaders in ways that address their concerns, but which also question policy, hold accountable dominant concepts and practices, and which enable the whole sector to discuss educational purposes and their relationship to outcomes as well as 'effectiveness'. Recent government policy has focused on promoting only research which suggests causal links between specific treatments and outcomes. It has taken 30 years for evidence based medicine to develop conceptual structures which have allowed for the broader recognition of different types of relationships between evidence and practice, so that research about whether a technique should be used rests on discussions of ethics, values, purposes, and the professional judgement of teachers. That is not the extent of the challenge for policy-makers, however. A vital test is their willingness to reform and innovate the accountability and regulation of schools, teaching and teacher education, as a necessary step to allow school leaders to more confidently take up their challenge.

For school leaders, the challenge laid out here is for space and resources to allow for the collective development of professional judgement and practice. Over and over again, these chapters outline the promise of collective discussion, decision making and critical evaluation in relation to professional development. We know that each of these, space and resources, are an enormous challenge, but we hope that curriculum reforms and a new Ofsted framework might begin to allow for at least the space for teachers to address research and practice in satisfying and intelligible ways.

For classroom teachers, the challenges are many, and we are aware that our ideas are jostled in a crowded market for teachers' attention, just as teachers themselves are hurried through their working days. We also recognise that we are asking teachers to think in ways that many of them will have been discouraged to during initial training and education, and which might go against the workplace pressures and even policies in which they are practising. We hope that in suggesting that teachers' own practice problems – the questions and dilemmas that they confront in teaching, are those which should have much more influence on the types and topics of research that are carried out, we will open up new possibilities for new relations between research and practice, researchers and practitioners and between practitioners.

For researchers who want to contribute to the practice of education, these chapters show a willingness to engage with research based on methodologies which do not directly dictate practice methods. However, some researchers and policy makers do not yet understand the role that different forms of research can make to education and are that means that some of us are far too quick to dismiss research which uses specific methodologies. We should all learn more about the contributions of methods beyond the ones we are comfortable with. We also need to make claims that recognise the limitations of our own methodologies and not fall into the temptation of over-promising or claiming impacts that cannot be supported by our methods or evidence. This implies a final related challenge for researchers: we need to work in ways that speak to researchers from different backgrounds, as well as to practitioners. Perhaps we can work in teams that provide that cross-disciplinary or cross-method expertise, or focus on problems or issues that other disciplines or methods have looked at, but in ways that provide novel perspectives or directions for further work. Finally, we also have to widen our conceptions about who can contribute to this work. Teachers should be consulted on research focusses and topics, but they can and should contribute as researchers in the ways we have suggested in this book.

ABOUT THE EDITORS

Megan Stephenson is an Associate Professor in Professional Practice at Leeds Trinity University. Her roles at LTU have included Primary PGCE Programme Lead, Early Reading and Phonics Curriculum Coordinator, and Academic Partnership Lead. She has a growing set of published works across her field of expertise. With Angela Gill, she recently published the core text for ITT trainees *Training to be a Primary School Teacher: ITT and Beyond*. Prior to working in HEI, she taught for over 20 years in primary provision across the North of England. She is currently studying for a professional Doctorate in Education at York St John University, where she is researching teacher education policy reform and social justice.

Angela Gill is an Associate Professor at Durham University. She is the Deputy Director of the Centre for CPD and Outreach in the School of Education. Whilst working at ITT, she was the Director of ITT Programmes, leading both UG and PGCE Programmes in the School of Education. With Megan Stephenson, she recently published the core text for ITT trainees *Training to be a Primary School Teacher: ITT and Beyond*. She is the Subject Lead for Primary English, and her areas of interest include phonics and writing. She is currently researching how play-based approaches can support the writing process in primary school. She has written and edited books and articles about many aspects of Primary English and the wider curriculum, and her recent publications include the fourth edition of *Teaching Systematic Synthetic Phonics in the Primary School* and the second edition of *Mastering Writing at Greater Depth*. She has presented at national conferences in the UK and has organised conferences for trainees related to key aspects of the curriculum, such as phonics and employability. For more than 20 years, she taught in primary schools in Durham and Somerset, during which time she was the Subject Lead for English and phonics.

Ed Podesta is an Associate Professor in Professional Practice at Leeds Trinity University. He taught history for 10 years in state schools, during which time he wrote school history textbooks and became head of a large history department in a school in Reading. He then took a career break to study for an MSc in Education Research Methods at the University of Leeds, after which he joined Leeds Trinity University, lecturing on undergraduate and postgraduate degrees and QTS programmes. For six years, he led the Secondary PGCE Department and now works with Megan Stephenson in helping colleagues who have moved from schooling to HE develop a scholarly practice and identity. He teaches on MA and PGCE modules, with a focus on research methods, inclusion and contemporary issues in education. He also leads on the University's QTS partnerships programme, which sees him teaching PGCert modules with partner QTS providers in the North of England. He has contributed chapters to books about teaching History and Science, and with Leigh Hoath edited *Professional Studies for Secondary Teaching*, a core textbook for secondary QTS programmes. Currently studying for a PhD at the University of Leeds, focused on the curriculum agency and autonomy of secondary teachers of English in England, he promises everyone that this is his last book before that PhD finally gets written.

ABOUT THE CONTRIBUTORS

Heena Dave is an Economic and Social Research Council (ESRC), Scottish Graduate School of Social Science-funded PhD researcher at the University of Stirling. Her research explores how school leaders create enabling conditions for climate change education in schools, enabling meaningful and lasting change for children and young people. In addition to her academic work, she is the Co-Founder of Climate Adapted Pathways for Education (CAPE), a charity that brings together researchers, educators, schools, and partners across the UK who are working to deliver high-quality climate change education. Previously, she worked as a Secondary Science Teacher and Educator.

Alison Griffiths has worked in education since 1992, holding a variety of roles across primary schools and higher education. She began her career as a class teacher, year leader, and literacy co-ordinator in primary schools in North Wales and London before moving into teacher education. Over the years, she has gained extensive experience in higher education, working at three universities where she has taken on roles, such as literacy tutor, module leader, programme leader, and head of teacher education. Currently, she serves as Deputy Head of School at Leeds Trinity University, overseeing the primary Post Graduate Certificate in Education (PGCE) programme. Throughout her career, she has engaged in a wide range of research projects, including studies on how universities can best support student teachers transitioning to work in areas of high diversity and the role of contemporary art in teacher education. She holds a Master's degree in the Arts and

Creativity and is in the final stages of completing her Professional Doctorate in Education. Her current research focuses on the intellectual and academic work of teacher educators, creative research methodologies, and the evolving notions of professional identity.

Leigh Hoath is a Professor of Science Education at Leeds Trinity University. With Ed Podesta, she recently published the core text for ITT trainees' *Professional Studies for Secondary Teachers* and with Ben Rogers *Primary Science in a Nutshell*, as well as many other books across the primary and secondary age phases. She has recently been Chair of the Association for Science Education, is a former Editor of their flagship journal *Primary Science* and is currently Editor of the journal *Practice: Contemporary Issues in Education*. She is Co-Founder of the charity Climate Adapted Pathways for Education (CAPE), which aims to equip teachers and school leaders with the knowledge and skills to help all children and young people take climate action and protect the environment.

Jo Hopton is an experienced practitioner across mainstream (primary and secondary) and FE. She moved into teacher education in 2014. In higher education she has worked in a range of settings, including university provision in FE colleges where her roles have included maths tutor, module lead, and programme lead. As Deputy Head of School at Leeds Trinity University, she oversees the Primary Undergraduate Programme. Her Masters in Education Research focused on the impact of mathematics anxiety on trainee teachers' self-efficacy. Her other research interests include widening participation and social mobility.

Evan McCormick is a Lecturer in Primary Education at Leeds Trinity University, with specialisms in Early Years and English. Prior to working in higher education, he had a successful career as an Early Years teacher and leader, additionally being involved in school improvement at multi-academy trust level. He is currently a PhD candidate at Lancaster University, where his research centres on interpretations and applications of LGBTQ+ picture books.

About the Contributors

Dr Amanda Nuttall is an Associate Professor in the School of Education at Leeds Trinity University. Whilst working in ITT, she has led both UG and PGCE programmes in primary education. Her doctoral thesis was focused on building a rich understanding of how teachers experience transitions and revisions in their identity[ies] as they engage in Master's level research activity. This work was influenced by her own experiences as a research-active teacher, alongside recent work in developing critical research literacy within initial and continuing teacher education programmes. Her broader research interests and publications include examining social justice in schooling and teacher education, teachers' critical research and knowledge creation work, and theorising professional development for educators in relation to notions of gender and class identity[ies].

Aimee Quickfall is the Head of the School of Education at Leeds Trinity University, where she is lucky enough to work with expert teacher educators and researchers, as well as inspiring students. Her research interests include well-being and workload in education, initial teacher education policy, and the experiences of academics, mentors, and teacher trainees, as well as feminist methodologies and approaches and research ethics.

Suzanne Tomlinson is the Programme Lead for the Leeds SCITT PGCE Secondary Programme and a Lead Partner of Leeds Trinity University. With a background in senior leadership roles within schools, she has extensive experience in Initial Teacher Education (ITE) and Teaching & Learning. Her current professional interests are focused on supporting trainees with Autism Spectrum Disorder (ASD) and providing mentorship and development opportunities for teachers in schools.

Samantha Wilkes is a Senior Lecturer at Leeds Trinity University, working across both the Postgraduate and Undergraduate Primary Education Programmes. She has extensive experience in the Early Years and KS1 curricula, with a particular focus on language development and acquisition as well as early reading and writing. Much of her work has been centred around the delivery of systematic synthetic phonics. Prior to working in higher education, she was a Head of School and mentored numerous early career teachers. Through this, her interest in teacher well-being and retention has led to both an MA in Education and currently an EdD, part-time. Her recent research centred around teacher identity, has made links to the retention of teachers and the role of ITE and schools within this.

Dr Charlotte Wright is a Senior Lecturer in Education, Programme Lead for the Secondary English PGCE and Programme Co-ordinator for the MA in Education at Leeds Trinity University. She has taught English for three decades in a range of schools and trains new teachers and teacher-researchers. Her own research interests include issues of inclusion and social justice in the English curriculum in secondary schools, the pedagogy of literary analysis and how it positions students and teachers, and identity development in teacher-researchers.

www.ingramcontent.com/pod-product-compliance
Lightning Source LLC
Chambersburg PA
CBHW051117230426
43667CB00014B/2616